LEARN TO

Crochet Decorative Edgings

Beaded Chain Lace Edging, page 100

www.companyscoming.com
visit our website

Mile-a-Minute Edging, page 116

Learn to Crochet Decorative Edgings

Copyright © Company's Coming Publishing Limited

First Printing April 2012

Library and Archives Canada Cataloguing in Publication
Learn to crochet decorative edgings.
(Workshop series)
Includes index.
ISBN 978-1-897477-75-5
1. Crocheting. 2. Borders, Ornamental (Decorative arts).
I. Title: Crochet decorative edgings. II. Series: Workshop series (Edmonton, Alta.)
TT820.L395 2012   746.43'2   C2011-906149-X

Published by
Company's Coming Publishing Limited
2311-96 Street
Edmonton, Alberta, Canada T6N 1G3
Tel: 780-450-6223 Fax: 780-450-1857
www.companyscoming.com

Company's Coming is a registered trademark owned by Company's Coming Publishing Limited

Printed in China

The Company's Coming Story

Jean Paré grew up with an understanding that family, friends and home cooking are the key ingredients for a good life. A mother of four, Jean worked as a professional caterer for 18 years, operating out of her home kitchen. During that time, she came to appreciate quick and easy recipes that call for everyday ingredients. In answer to mounting requests for her recipes, Company's Coming cookbooks were born, and Jean moved on to a new chapter in her career.

In the beginning, Jean worked from a spare bedroom in her home, located in the small prairie town of Vermilion, Alberta, Canada. The first Company's Coming cookbook, *150 Delicious Squares*, was an immediate bestseller. Today, with well over 150 titles in print, Company's Coming has earned the distinction of publishing Canada's most popular cookbooks. The company continues to gain new supporters by adhering to Jean's "Golden Rule of Cooking"—Never share a recipe you wouldn't use yourself. It's an approach that has worked—millions of times over!

Company's Coming cookbooks are distributed throughout Canada, the United States, Australia and other international English-language markets. French and Spanish language editions have also been published. Sales to date have surpassed 30 million copies with no end in sight. Familiar and trusted in home kitchens around the world, Company's Coming cookbooks are highly regarded both as kitchen workbooks and as family heirlooms.

Company's Coming founder Jean Paré

Just as Company's Coming continues to promote the tradition of home cooking, the same is now true with crafting. Like good cooking, great craft results depend upon easy-to-follow instructions, readily available materials and enticing photographs of the finished products. Also like cooking, crafting is meant to be enjoyed in the home or cottage. Company's Coming Crafts, then, is a natural extension from the kitchen into the family room or den.

Because Company's Coming operates a test kitchen and not a craft shop, we've partnered with a major North American craft content publisher to assemble a variety of craft compilations exclusively for us. Our editors have been involved every step of the way. You can see the excellent results for yourself in the book you're holding.

Company's Coming Crafts are for everyone—whether you're a beginner or a seasoned pro. What better gift could you offer than something you've made yourself? In these hectic days, people still enjoy crafting parties; they bring family and friends together in the same way a good meal does. Company's Coming is proud to support crafters with this new creative book series.

We hope you enjoy these easy-to-follow, informative and colourful books, and that they inspire your creativity. So, don't delay—get crafty!

TABLE OF CONTENTS

Foreword 7 • Crochet Basics 8

Rib Edgings

Add a textured linear look with these ribbed edgings.

Fringe Edgings

These ornamental edgings are fun and add a unique look to your designs.

Knit-Look Dishcloth, page 46

Poncho Doll Fringe Scarf, page 68

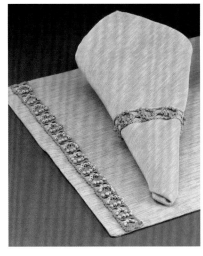

Narrow Beaded Fan Lace Edging, page 104

TABLE OF CONTENTS

Ruffle Edgings

Ruffles add frill and femininity to spice up your designs.

Beaded Edgings

Add extra bling to your design with a beaded edging.

Edgings & Insertions

Embellish your home and fashion decor with these exquisite edgings and insertions.

Pretty in Pink
Baby Blanket,
page 79

Lampshade Edgings, page 108

Rows of Pineapples, page 113

Make it yourself!

CRAFT WORKSHOP SERIES

Get a craft class in a book! General instructions teach basic skills or how to apply them in a new way. Easy-to-follow steps, diagrams and photos make projects simple.

Whether paper crafting, knitting, crocheting, beading, sewing or quilting—find beautiful, fun designs you can make yourself.

COLLECT THEM ALL!

Kids Learn To Knit, Quilt And Crochet
Learn To Bead Earrings
Learn To Bead Jewellery
Learn To Craft With Paper
Learn To Crochet For Baby
Learn To Crochet In A Day
Learn To Knit For Baby
Learn To Knit In The Round
Learn To Knit Socks
Learn To Make Cards With Folds
Learn To Make Cards With Photos
Learn To Quilt Fat Quarters
Learn To Quilt With Panels
Learn To Sew For The Table

FOREWORD

Learn to Crochet Decorative Edgings is a book that will take your creativity to new heights! Written in a clear, easy-to-follow style, it is filled with beautiful colour photographs of over 50 different edgings plus 14 creative designs showing how to use edgings. Whether the edging is used to embellish a crochet design or a purchased item, it can turn an ordinary project into a spectacular one.

Projects include a fun Poncho Doll Fringe Scarf made using adorable little yarn dolls as the fringe, a Pretty in Pink Baby Blanket edged in pretty ruffles for your favourite little girl, a beaded edging that adds a touch of fanciness to an ordinary lampshade, and plain dish towels that are made special with a simple edging. Also included is a beautiful pineapple insertion that adds elegance to a purchased tablecloth or pillowcase.

You will find an exciting variety of unique and unusual edgings, including ribs, fringe, ruffles, insertions, florals and beads. All of the edgings can be made using yarn or thread—just experiment with hook sizes to get the gauge you want.

The edging possibilities are endless. You can remake your wardrobe and add pizzazz to your home decor, or make a quick gift that will be treasured because it's original and homemade! Be creative and have fun simply by adding an edging.

As an added bonus, this book includes the basics of crochet stitches that can be used as a refresher or to expand your crochet knowledge. There are great tips on yarn types, hook sizes, how to check your gauge and how to read patterns. You'll love the step-by-step illustrations and photos. Seasoned pros and beginners alike will refer to these basic instructions time after time.

No matter what your taste—whimsical, frilly, sophisticated or traditional—you are sure to find an edging that fits your own style and skill level.

Narrow Shell Lace Edging, page 102

CROCHET BASICS

Triangles in Lace, page 110

Yarns

Both yarn and crochet cottons come in many sizes, from the fine crochet cotton used for doilies to the wonderful bulky mohair used for afghans and sweaters. The most commonly used yarn is medium (or worsted) weight. It is readily available in a wide variety of beautiful colours, and is the weight we will use in our lessons. Always read yarn labels carefully. The label will tell you how much yarn is in the skein, hank or ball in ounces, grams, metres and/or yards. Read the label to find out the fibre content of the yarn, the yarn's washability, and sometimes how to pull the yarn from the skein. There is also usually a dye-lot number on the label. The dye-lot number assures you that the colour of each skein with this number is the same. Yarn of the same colour name may vary in shade somewhat from dye lot to dye lot, creating variations in colour when a project is completed. Therefore, when purchasing yarn for a project, it is important to match the dye-lot numbers on the skeins, and buy all the yarn you need to complete a project at the same time.

Tapestry Needle

You'll need a tapestry needle—a blunt-pointed sewing needle with an eye big enough to carry the yarn—for weaving in yarn ends and sewing seams. A size 16 steel tapestry needle works well. You can buy big plastic needles called yarn needles, but they are not as good as the steel needles.

Gauge

Gauge is the single most important factor in crochet. If you don't work to gauge, your crocheted projects may not be the correct size, and you may not have enough yarn to finish your project.

Gauge means the number of stitches per inch, and number of rows per inch, that result from a specified yarn worked with a specified-sized hook. Since everyone crochets differently—loosely, tightly or in-between—the measurements of individual work can vary greatly even when using the same-sized hook and yarn. It is your responsibility to make sure you achieve the gauge specified in the pattern.

Hook sizes given in the materials lists are merely guides and should never be used without making a 4-inch-square sample swatch to check gauge. Make the sample gauge swatch using the hook size, yarn and stitch specified in the pattern. If you have more stitches per inch than specified, try again using a larger-sized hook. If you have fewer stitches per inch than specified, try again using a smaller-sized hook. Do not hesitate to change to a larger- or smaller-sized hook, if necessary, to achieve gauge.

If you have the correct number of stitches per inch, but cannot achieve the row gauge, adjust the height of your stitches. This means that after inserting the hook to begin a new stitch, draw up a little more yarn if your stitches are not tall enough—this makes the first loop slightly higher—or draw up less yarn if your stitches are too tall. Practice will help you achieve the correct height.

This photo shows how to measure your gauge:

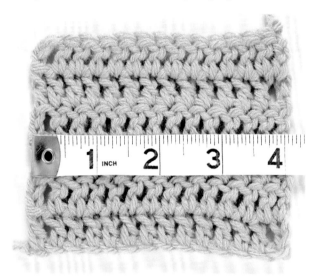

Reading Patterns

Crochet patterns are written in a special language full of abbreviations, asterisks, parentheses, brackets and other symbols and terms. These short forms are used so that instructions will not take up too much space. They may seem confusing at first, but once understood, they are easy to follow.

Abbreviations

beg begin/begins/beginning
bpdc back post double crochet
bpsc back post single crochet
bptr back post treble crochet
CC contrasting colour
ch(s) chain stitch(es)
ch- refers to chain or space previously made
     (i.e. ch-1 space)
ch sp(s) chain space(s)
cl(s) cluster(s)
cm centimetre(s)
dc double crochet (singular/plural)
dc dec double crochet 2 or more stitches together,
     as indicated
dec decrease/decreases/decreasing
dtr double treble crochet
ext extended
fpdc front post double crochet
fpsc front post single crochet
fptr front post treble crochet
g gram(s)
hdc half double crochet
hdc dec half double crochet 2 or more stitches together,
     as indicated
inc increase/increases/increasing
lp(s) loop(s)

MC main colour
mm millimetre(s)
oz ounce(s)
pc popcorn(s)
rem remain/remains/remaining
rep(s) repeat(s)
rnd(s) round(s)
RS right side
sc single crochet
sc dec single crochet 2 or more stitches together,
     as indicated
sk skip/skipped/skipping
sl st(s) slip stitch(es)
sp(s) space(s)/spaced
st(s) stitch(es)
tog together
tr treble crochet
trtr triple treble crochet
WS wrong side
yd(s) yard(s)
yo yarn over

Symbols

* An asterisk is used to mark the beginning of a portion of instructions which will be worked more than once; thus, "rep from * twice" means after working the instructions once, repeat the instructions following the asterisk twice more (3 times in all).

[ ] Brackets are used to enclose instructions which should be repeated the number of times specified immediately following the brackets: "[2 sc in next dc, sc in next dc] twice." Brackets are also used to indicate additional or clarifying information for multiple sizes: "child's size 2 [4, 6]"; "Row 29 [31, 33]."

( ) Parentheses are used to set off and clarify a group of stitches that are to be worked all into the same space or stitch, such as: "in corner sp work (2 dc, ch 1, 2 dc)."

{ } Braces are used to indicate a set of repeat instructions within a bracketed or parenthetical set of repeat instructions: "[{ch 5, sc in next ch sp} twice, ch 5, sk next dc]"; "({dc, ch 1} 5 times, dc) in next ch sp)."

Terms
Front loop (front lp) is the loop toward you at the top of the stitch.

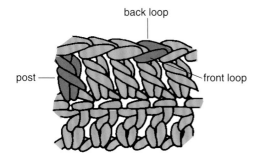

Back loop (back lp) is the loop away from you at the top of the stitch.

Post is the vertical part of the stitch.

Wrong side (WS): the side of the work that will not show when project is in use.

Right side (RS): the side that will show.

Right-hand side: the side nearest your right hand as you are working.

Left-hand side: the side nearest your left hand as you are working.

Right front: the piece of a garment that will be worn on the right-hand side of the body.

Left front: the piece of a garment that will be worn on the left-hand side of the body.

How To Hold Your Hook

Crochet hooks come in many sizes, from very fine steel hooks used to make intricate doilies and lace to very large ones of plastic or wood used to make bulky sweaters or rugs.

The hooks you will use most often are made of aluminum, about 6 inches long and sized alphabetically by letter from B (the smallest) to K. For our lessons, you'll need a size H hook, which is a medium size.

The aluminum crochet hook looks like this:

In Figure 1, (A) is the hook end, which is used to hook the yarn and draw it through other loops of yarn (called stitches). (B) is the throat, a shaped area that helps you slide the stitch up onto (C), the working area. (D) is the fingerhold, a flattened area that helps you grip the hook comfortably, usually with your thumb and third finger. (E) is the handle, which rests under your fourth and little fingers, and provides balance for easy, smooth work.

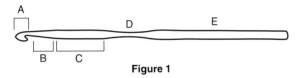

Figure 1

It is important that every stitch is made on the working area, never on the throat (which would make the stitch too tight) and never on the fingerhold (which would stretch the stitch).

The hook is held in the right hand, with the thumb and third finger on the fingerhold, and the index finger near the tip of the hook (Figure 2).

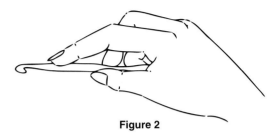

Figure 2

The hook should be turned slightly toward you, not facing up or down. Figure 3 shows how the hook is held, viewing from underneath the hand. The hook should be held firmly, but not tightly.

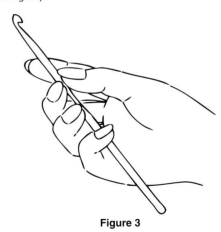

Figure 3

Lesson 1: Chain Stitch (ch)

Crochet usually begins with a series of chain stitches called a beginning, starting or foundation chain. Begin by making a slip knot on the hook about 6 inches from the free end of the yarn. Loop the yarn as shown in Figure 4.

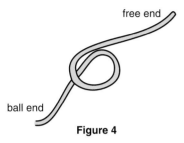

free end

ball end

Figure 4

Insert the hook through centre of loop and hook the free end (Figure 5).

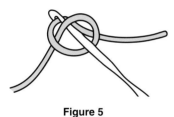

Figure 5

Pull the free end through the loop and up onto the working area of the hook (Figure 6).

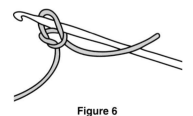

Figure 6

Pull the free yarn end to tighten the loop (Figure 7).

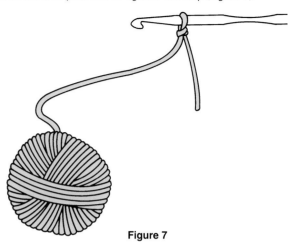

Figure 7

The loop should be firm, but loose enough to slide back and forth easily on the hook. Be sure you still have about a 6-inch yarn end.

Hold the hook, now with its slip knot, in your right hand (Figure 8).

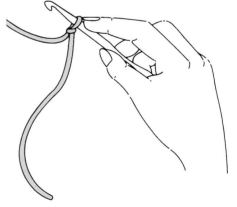

Figure 8

Now let's make the first chain stitch.

1. Hold the base of the slip knot with the thumb and index finger of your left hand, and thread yarn from the skein over your middle finger (Figure 9a) and under the remaining fingers of your left hand (Figure 9b).

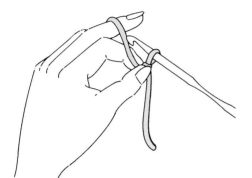

Figure 9a

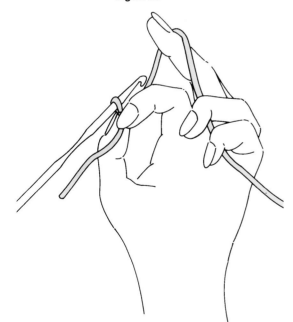

Figure 9b

Your middle finger will stick up a bit to help the yarn feed smoothly from the skein; the other fingers help maintain even tension on the yarn as you work.

Tip: As you practice, you can adjust the way your left hand holds the yarn or thread to however is most comfortable for you.

2. Bring the yarn over the hook from back to front and hook it (Figure 10).

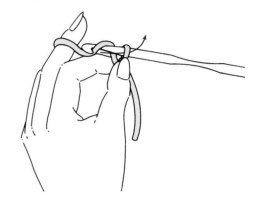

Figure 10

Draw hooked yarn through the loop of the slip knot on the hook and up onto the working area of the hook *(see arrow on Figure 10)*; you have now made one chain stitch (Figure 11).

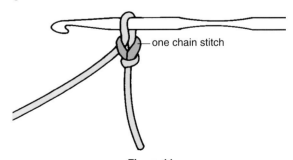

—one chain stitch

Figure 11

3. Again bring the yarn over the hook from back to front (Figure 12a).

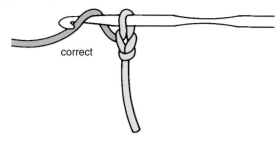

correct

Figure 12a

Tip: Take care not to bring yarn from front to back (Figure 12b).

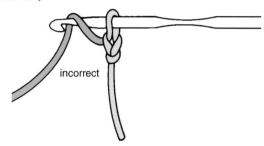

incorrect

Figure 12b

Hook it and draw through loop on the hook—you have made another chain stitch (Figure 13).

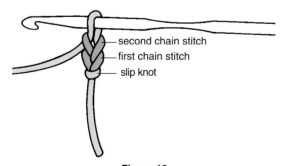

second chain stitch
first chain stitch
slip knot

Figure 13

Repeat step 3 for each additional chain stitch, being careful to move your left thumb and index finger up the chain close to the hook after each new stitch or two (Figure 14a). This helps you control the work.

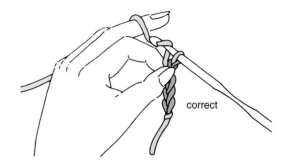

correct

Figure 14a

Tip: Figure 14b shows the incorrect way to hold the stitches. Also be sure to pull each new stitch up onto the working area of the hook.

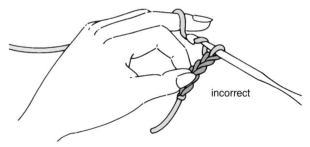

incorrect

Figure 14b

The working yarn and the work in progress are always held in your left hand.

Practice making chains until you are comfortable with your grip of the hook and the flow of the yarn. In the beginning your work will be uneven, with some chain stitches loose and others tight. While you're learning, try to keep the chain stitches loose. As your skill increases, the chain should be firm, but not tight, with all chain stitches even in size.

Tip: As you practice, if the hook slips out of a stitch, don't get upset! Just insert the hook again from the front into the centre of the last stitch, taking care not to twist the loop (Figure 15).

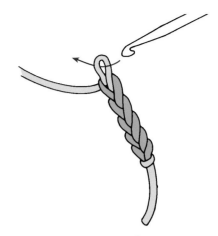

Figure 15

When you are comfortable with the chain stitch, draw your hook out of the last stitch and pull out the work back to the beginning. Now you've learned the important first step of crochet: the beginning or foundation chain.

Lesson 2: Working Into the Chain

Once you have worked the beginning chain, you are ready to begin the stitches required to make any project. These stitches are worked into the foundation chain. For practice, make six chain stitches loosely.

Tip: When counting your chain stitches at the start of a pattern—which you must do very carefully before continuing—note that the loop on the hook is never counted as a stitch, and the starting slip knot is never counted as a stitch (Figure 16).

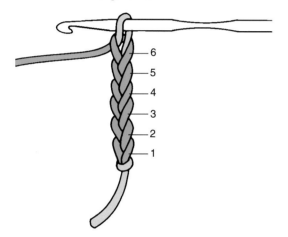

Figure 16

Now stop and look at the chain. The front looks like a series of interlocking V's (Figure 16), and each stitch has a bump or bar at the back (Figure 17).

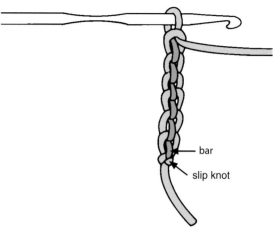

bar

slip knot

Figure 17

You will never work into the first chain from the hook. Depending on the stitch, you will work into the second, third, fourth, etc., chain from the hook. The instructions will always state how many chains to skip before starting the first stitch.

When working a stitch, insert hook from the front of the chain, through the centre of a V at the top of the chain and under the corresponding bar on the back of the same chain (Figure 18a).

Excluding the first stitch, you will work into every stitch in the chain unless the pattern states differently, but not into the starting slip knot (Figure 18b). Be sure that you do not skip that last chain at the end.

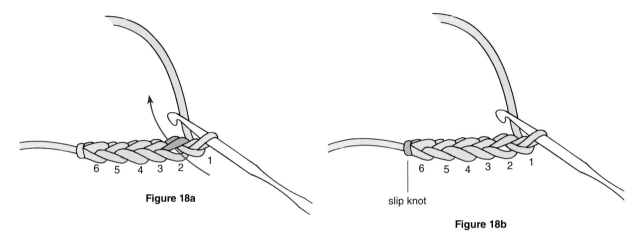

Figure 18a

Figure 18b

Lesson 3: Single Crochet (sc)

Most crochet fabric is made with variations on just four different stitches: single crochet, double crochet, half double crochet and treble crochet. The stitches differ mainly in height, which is varied by the number of times the yarn is wrapped around the hook. The shortest and most basic of these stitches is the single crochet.

Working Row 1

To practice, begin with the chain of six stitches made in Lesson 2 and work the first row of single crochet as follows:

1. Skip first chain stitch from hook. Insert hook in the second chain stitch through the centre of the V and under the back bar; with third finger of your left hand, bring yarn over the hook from back to front and hook the yarn (Figure 19).

Figure 19

Draw yarn through the chain stitch and well up onto the working area of the hook (Figure 19). You now have two loops on the hook (Figure 20).

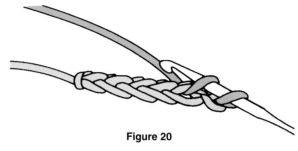

Figure 20

2. Again, bring yarn over the hook from back to front, hook the yarn and draw it through both loops on the hook (Figure 21).

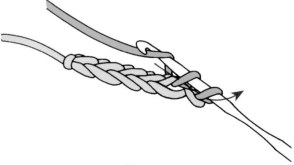

Figure 21

One loop will remain on the hook, and you have made one single crochet (Figure 22).

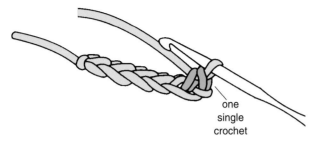

one
single
crochet

Figure 22

3. Insert hook in next chain stitch as before, hook the yarn and draw it through the chain stitch; hook the yarn again and draw it through both loops: You have made another single crochet.

Repeat Step 3 in each remaining chain stitch, taking care to work in the last chain stitch, but not in the slip knot. You have completed one row of single crochet, and should have five stitches in the row. Figure 23 shows how to count the stitches.

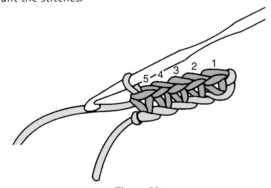

Figure 23

Tip: As you work, be careful not to twist the chain; keep all the V's facing you.

Working Row 2

To work the second row of single crochet, you need to turn the work in the direction of the arrow (counterclockwise), as shown in Figure 24a, so you can work back across the first row.

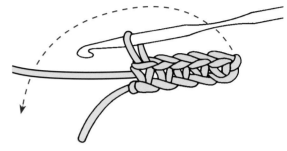

Figure 24a

Do not remove the hook from the loop as you do this (Figure 24b).

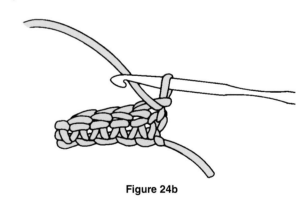

Figure 24b

Now you need to bring the yarn up to the correct height to work the first stitch. So, to raise the yarn, chain one (this is called a beginning chain).

This row, and all the following rows of single crochet, will be worked into a previous row of single crochet, not into the starting chain as you did before. Remember that when you worked into the starting chain, you inserted the hook through the centre of the V and under the bar. This is only done when working into a starting chain.

To work into a previous row of crochet, insert the hook under both loops of the previous stitch, as shown in Figure 25, instead of through the centre of the V.

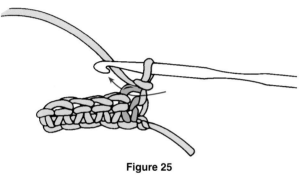

Figure 25

The first single crochet of the row is worked in the last stitch of the previous row (Figure 25), not into the beginning chain. Work a single crochet into each single crochet to the end, taking care to work in each stitch, especially the last stitch, which is easy to miss (Figure 26).

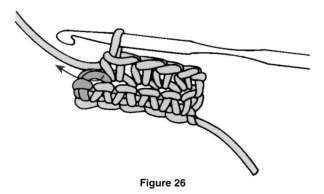

Figure 26

Stop now and count your stitches; you should still have five single crochet on the row (Figure 27).

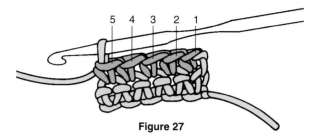

Figure 27

Tip: When you want to pause to count stitches, check your work, have a snack or chat on the phone, you can remove your hook from the work—but do this at the end of a row, not in the middle. To remove the hook, pull straight up on the hook to make a long loop (Figure 28). Then withdraw the hook and put it on a table or other safe place (sofas and chairs have a habit of eating crochet hooks). Put work in a safe place so that the loop is not pulled out. To begin work again, just insert the hook in the big loop (don't twist the loop), and pull on the yarn from the ball to tighten the loop.

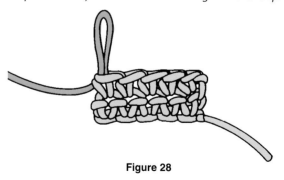

Figure 28

To end row 2, after the last single crochet, turn the work counterclockwise.

Here is the way instructions for row 2 might be written in a pattern:

Row 2: Ch 1, sc in each sc, turn.

Note: To save space, a number of abbreviations are used. For a list of abbreviations used in patterns, see page 10.

Working Row 3

Row 3 is worked exactly as you worked row 2. Here are the instructions as they would be given in a pattern:

Row 3: Rep row 2.

Now wasn't that easy? For practice, work three more rows, which means you will repeat row 2 three times more.

Tip: Try to keep your stitches as smooth and even as possible; remember to work loosely rather than tightly and to make each stitch well up on the working area of the hook. Be sure to turn at the end of each row and to check carefully to be sure you've worked into the last stitch of each row.

Count the stitches at the end of each row; do you still have five? Good work.

Tip: What if you don't have five stitches at the end of a row? Perhaps you worked two stitches in one stitch or skipped a stitch. Find your mistake, then just pull out your stitches back to the mistake. Pulling out in crochet is simple—just take out the hook and gently pull on the yarn. The stitches will come out easily; when you reach the place where you want to start again, insert the hook in the last loop (taking care not to twist it) and begin.

Fastening Off

It's time to move on to another stitch, so let's fasten off your single crochet practice piece, which you can keep for future reference. After the last stitch of the last row, cut the yarn, leaving a 6-inch end. As you did when you took your hook out for a break, draw the hook straight up, but this time draw the cut end of the yarn completely through the stitch. Photo A shows an actual sample of six rows of single crochet to which you can compare your practice rows. It also shows how to count the stitches and rows.

Photo A

Now you can put the piece away, and it won't pull out (you might want to tag this piece as a sample of single crochet).

Lesson 4: Double Crochet (dc)

Double crochet is a taller stitch than single crochet. To practice, first chain 14 stitches loosely. Then work the first row of double crochet as follows:

Working Row 1

1. Bring yarn once over the hook from back to front (as though you were going to make another chain stitch); skip the first three chains from the hook, and then insert hook in the fourth chain (Figure 29).

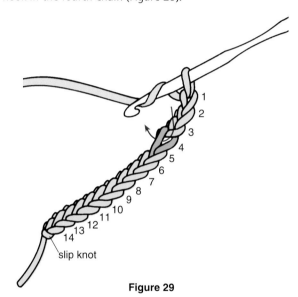

Figure 29

Remember not to count the loop on the hook as a chain. Be sure to go through the centre of the V of the chain and under the bar at the back, and do not twist the chain.

2. Hook yarn and draw it through the chain stitch and up onto the working area of the hook: you now have three loops on the hook (Figure 30).

Figure 30

3. Hook yarn and draw through the first two loops on the hook (Figure 31).

Figure 31

You now have two loops on the hook (Figure 32).

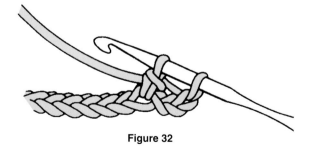

Figure 32

4. Hook yarn and draw through both loops on the hook (Figure 33).

Figure 33

You have now completed one double crochet and one loop remains on the hook (Figure 34).

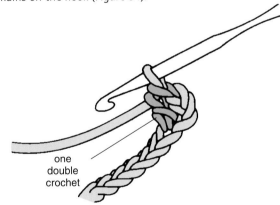

one
double
crochet

Figure 34

Repeat steps 1 through 4 in each chain stitch across (except in step 1, work in next chain stitch; don't skip three chains).

When you've worked a double crochet in the last chain, pull out your hook and look at your work. Then count your double crochet stitches. There should be 12 of them, counting the first three chain stitches you skipped at the beginning of the row as a double crochet (Figure 35).

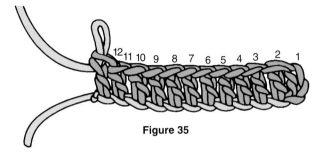

Figure 35

Tip: In working double crochet on a beginning chain row, the three chains skipped before making the first double crochet are always counted as a double crochet stitch.

Turn the work counterclockwise before beginning row 2.

Working Row 2

To work row 2, you need to bring the yarn up to the correct height for the next row. To raise the yarn, chain three (this is called the beginning chain).

The three chains in the beginning chain that was just made count as the first double crochet of the new row, so skip the first double crochet and work a double crochet in the second stitch. Be sure to insert the hook under the top two loops of the stitch: Figures 36a and 36b indicate the correct and incorrect placement of this stitch.

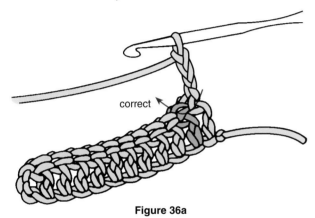

Figure 36a

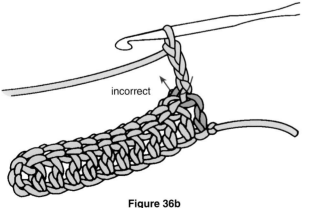

Figure 36b

Work a double crochet in each remaining stitch across the previous row; at the end of each row, be sure to work the last double crochet in the top of the beginning chain from the previous row. Be sure to insert the hook in the centre of the V (and back bar) of the top chain of the beginning chain (Figure 37). Stop and count your double crochet stitches; there should be 12 stitches. Now, turn the rows.

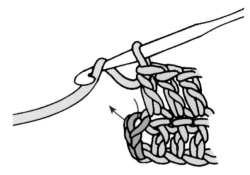

Figure 37

Here is the way the instructions might be written in a pattern:

Row 2: Ch 3, dc in each dc across, turn. *(12 dc)*

Working Row 3

Row 3 is worked exactly as you worked row 2.

In a pattern, instructions would read:

Row 3: Rep row 2.

For practice, work three more rows, repeating row 2. At the end of the last row, fasten off the yarn as you did for the single crochet practice piece. Photo B shows a sample of six rows of double crochet and how to count the stitches and rows.

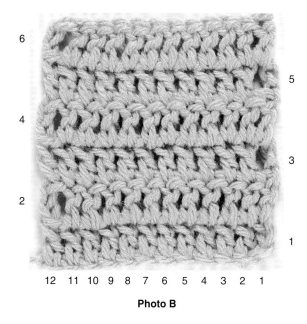

6

5

4

3

2

1

12 11 10 9 8 7 6 5 4 3 2 1

Photo B

Break Time!

Now you have learned the two most-often-used stitches in crochet. Since you've worked so hard, it's time to take a break. Walk around, relax your hands, have a snack or just take a few minutes to release the stress that sometimes develops when learning something new.

Lesson 5: Half Double Crochet (hdc)

Just as its name implies, this stitch eliminates one step of double crochet and works up about half as tall.

To practice, chain 13 stitches loosely.

Working Row 1

1. Bring yarn once over hook from back to front, skip the first two chains, and then insert hook in the third chain from the hook (Figure 38).

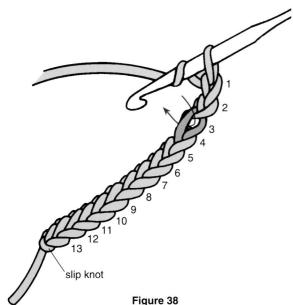

Figure 38

Remember not to count the loop on the hook as a chain.

2. Hook yarn and draw it through the chain stitch and up onto the working area of the hook. You now have three loops on the hook (Figure 39).

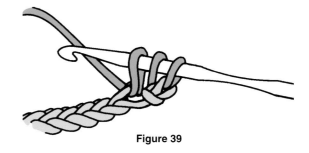

Figure 39

3. Hook yarn and draw it through all three loops on the hook in one motion (Figure 40).

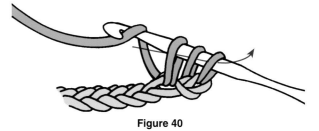

Figure 40

You have completed one half double crochet and one loop remains on the hook (Figure 41).

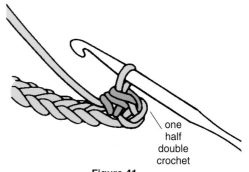

Figure 41

In next chain stitch, work a half double crochet as follows:

1. Bring yarn once over hook from back to front, insert hook in next chain.

2. Hook yarn and draw it through the chain stitch and up onto the working area of the hook. You now have three loops on the hook.

3. Hook yarn and draw it through all three loops on the hook in one motion.

Repeat the previous three steps in each remaining chain stitch across. Stop and count your stitches: You should have 12 half double crochet stitches, counting the first two chains you skipped at the beginning of the row as a half double crochet stitch (Figure 42).

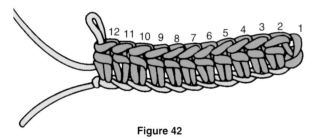

Figure 42

Turn your work.

Working Row 2

Like double crochet, the beginning chain counts as a stitch in half double crochet (unless your pattern specifies otherwise). Chain two, skip the first half double crochet stitch of the previous row and work a half double crochet stitch in the second stitch (Figure 43) and in each remaining stitch across the previous row. At the end of the row, turn.

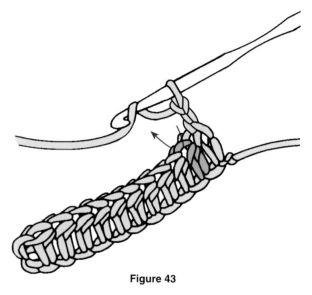

Figure 43

Here is the way the instructions might be written in a pattern:

Row 2: Ch 2, hdc in each hdc across, turn. *(12 hdc)*

Working Row 3

Row 3 is worked exactly as you worked row 2.

For practice, work three more rows, repeating row 2. Be sure to count your stitches carefully at the end of each row. When the practice rows are completed, fasten off. Photo C shows a sample of six rows of half double crochet stitches, and how to count the stitches and the rows.

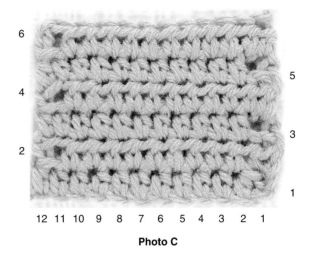

Photo C

Lesson 6: Treble Crochet (tr)

Treble crochet is a tall stitch that works up quickly and is fun to do. To practice, first chain 15 stitches loosely. Then work the first row as follows:

Working Row 1

1. Bring yarn twice over the hook (from back to front), skip the first four chains, and then insert hook into the fifth chain from the hook (Figure 44).

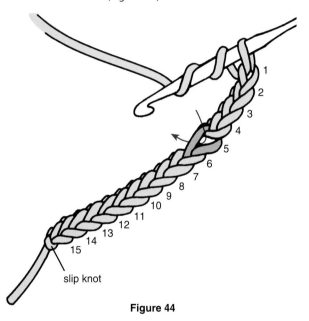

slip knot

Figure 44

2. Hook yarn and draw it through the chain stitch and up onto the working area of the hook; you now have four loops on the hook (Figure 45).

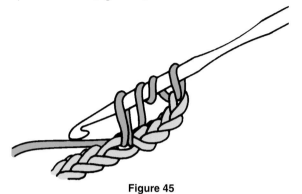

Figure 45

3. Hook yarn and draw it through the first two loops on the hook (Figure 46a).

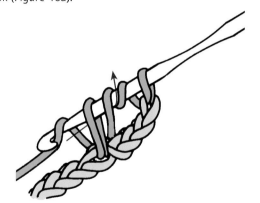

Figure 46a

You now have three loops on the hook (Figure 46b).

Figure 46b

4. Hook yarn again and draw it through the next two loops on the hook (Figure 47a).

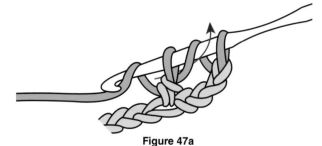

Figure 47a

Two loops remain on the hook (Figure 47b).

Figure 47b

5. Hook yarn and draw it through both remaining loops on the hook (Figure 48).

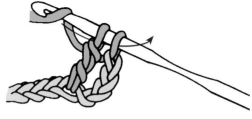

Figure 48

You have now completed one treble crochet, and one loop remains on the hook (Figure 49).

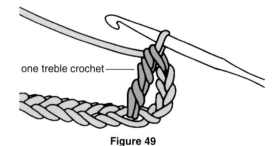

one treble crochet

Figure 49

In next chain stitch work a treble crochet as follows:

1. Bring yarn twice over the hook (from back to front); insert hook in the next chain (Figure 50).

Figure 50

2. Hook yarn and draw it through the chain stitch and up onto the working area of the hook; you now have four loops on the hook.

3. Hook yarn and draw it through the first two loops on the hook. You now have three loops on the hook.

4. Hook yarn again and draw it through the next two loops on the hook. Two loops remain on the hook.

5. Hook yarn and draw it through both remaining loops on the hook.

Repeat the previous five steps in each remaining chain stitch across.

When you've worked a treble crochet in the last chain, count your stitches. There should be 12 of them, counting the first four chains you skipped at the beginning of the row as a treble crochet (Figure 51); turn work.

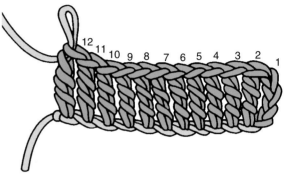

Figure 51

Tip: In working the first row of treble crochet, the four chains skipped before making the first treble crochet stitch are always counted as a treble crochet stitch.

Working Row 2

Chain four to bring your yarn up to the correct height, and to count as the first stitch of the row. Skip the first stitch and work a treble crochet in the 2nd stitch (Figure 52).

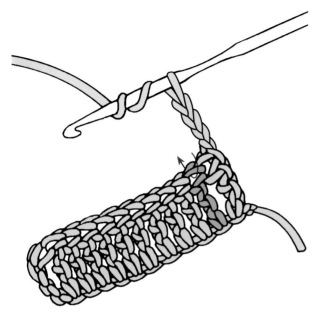

Figure 52

Work a treble crochet in each remaining stitch across previous row; be sure to work last treble crochet in the top of the beginning chain from the previous row. Count your stitches to be sure you still have 12 stitches; turn work.

Tip: Remember to work last treble crochet of each row in beginning chain of previous row. Missing this stitch in the beginning chain is a common error.

Here is the way the instructions might be written in a pattern:

Row 2: Ch 4, tr in each tr across, turn. *(12 tr)*

Working Row 3

Work row 3 exactly as you worked row 2.

For practice, work three more rows, repeating row 2. At the end of the last row, fasten off the yarn. Photo D shows a sample of six rows of treble crochet and how to count the stitches and rows.

Photo D

Lesson 7: Slip Stitch (sl st)

This is the shortest of all crochet stitches and is really more a technique than a stitch. Slip stitches are usually used to move yarn across a group of stitches without adding height, or they may be used to join different part of a project.

Moving Yarn Across Stitches
Chain 10.

Working Row 1
Double crochet in the fourth chain stitch from hook (see page 23) and in each chain stitch across. Turn work. On the next row you are going to slip stitch across the first four stitches before beginning to work double crochet again.

Working Row 2
Instead of making three chain stitches for the beginning chain as you would usually do for a second row of double crochet, this time just chain one. The beginning chain-1 does not count as a stitch; therefore, insert the hook under both loops of first stitch, hook yarn and draw it through both loops of stitch and loop on the hook (Figure 53)—one slip stitch made.

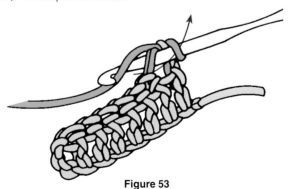

Figure 53

Work a slip stitch in the same manner in each of the next three stitches. Now we're going to finish the row in double crochet; chain three to get yarn at the right height (the chain-3 counts as a double crochet), and then work a double crochet in each of the remaining stitches. Look at your work and see how you moved the thread across with slip stitches, adding very little height (Figure 54).

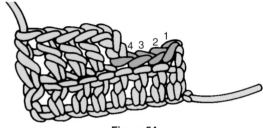

Figure 54

Fasten off and save the sample.

Here is the way the instructions might be written in a pattern:

Row 2: Ch 1, sl st in each of first 4 dc, ch 3, dc in each rem dc across, turn. *(5 dc)*

Fasten off.

Tip: When you slip-stitch across stitches, always work very loosely.

Joining Stitches

Joining a Chain Into a Circle
Chain six, and then insert hook through the first chain you made (next to the slip knot—Figure 55).

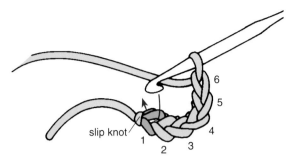

Figure 55

Hook yarn and draw it through the chain and through the loop on hook; you have now joined the six chains into a circle or a ring. This is the way many motifs, such as granny squares, are started. Cut yarn and keep this practice piece as a sample.

Joining the End of a Round to the Beginning of the Same Round

Chain six, join with a slip stitch in first chain you made to form a ring. Chain three, work 11 double crochet in the ring, insert hook in third chain of beginning chain-3 (Figure 56); hook yarn and draw it through the chain and through the loop on the hook; you have now joined the round. Cut yarn and keep this piece as a sample.

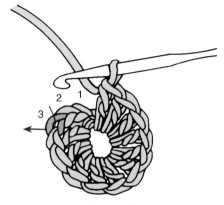

Figure 56

Here is the way the instructions might be written in a pattern:

Rnd 1: Ch 3, 11 dc in ring, join in 3rd ch of beg ch-3.

Lesson 8: Stitch Sampler

Now that you've learned the basic stitches of crochet, the hard part is over!

To help you understand the difference in the way single crochet, half double crochet, double crochet and treble crochet stitches are worked, and the difference in their heights, let's make one more sample.

Chain 17 stitches loosely. Taking care not to work too tightly, single crochet in the second chain from hook and in each of the next three chains; work a half double crochet in each of the next four chains; work a double crochet in each of the next four chains; work a treble crochet in each of the next four chains; fasten off. Your work should look like Photo E.

Photo E

Lesson 9: Working With Colours

Working with more than one colour often involves reading charts, changing colours and learning how to carry or pick up colours.

Working From Charts

Charts are easy to work from once you understand how to follow them. When working from a chart, remember that for each odd-numbered row, you will work the chart from right to left, and for each even-numbered row, you will work the chart from left to right.

Odd-numbered rows are worked on the right side of the piece and even-numbered rows are worked on the wrong side. To help follow across the row, you will find it helpful to place a ruler or sheet of paper directly below the row being worked.

Changing Colours

To change from the working colour to a new colour, work the last stitch to be done in the working colour until two loops remain on the hook (Photo F). Draw new colour through the two loops on hook. Drop working colour (Photo G) and continue to work in the new colour. This method can be used when change of colour is at the end of a row or within the row.

Photo F

Carrying or Picking Up Colours

In some patterns, you may need to carry a colour on the wrong side of the work for several stitches or pick up a colour used on the previous row. To carry a colour means to carry the strand on the wrong side of the work. To prevent having loops of unworked yarn, it is helpful to work over the strand of the carried colour. To do this, consider the strand a part of the stitch being worked into and simply insert the hook in the stitch and draw the new colour through (Photo H). When changing from working colour to a colour that has been carried or used on the previous row, always bring this colour under the working colour. This is very important, as it prevents holes in your work.

Photo G

Photo H

Lesson 10: Increasing & Decreasing

Shaping is done by increasing, which adds stitches to make the crocheted piece wider, or decreasing, which subtracts stitches to make the piece narrower.

Tip: Make a practice sample by chain stitching 15 stitches loosely and working four rows of single crochet with 14 stitches in each row. Do not fasten off at end of last row. Use this sample swatch to practice the following method of increasing stitches.

Increasing

To increase one stitch in single, half double, double or treble crochet, simply work two stitches in one stitch. For example, if you are working in single crochet and you need to increase one stitch, you would work one single crochet in the next stitch; then you would work another single crochet in the same stitch.

For practice: On sample swatch, turn work and chain one. Single crochet in first two stitches; increase in next stitch by working two single crochet in same stitch (Figure 57).

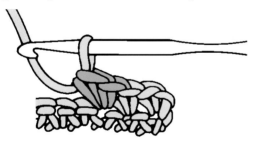

Figure 57
single crochet increase

Repeat increase in each stitch across row to last two stitches; single crochet in each of next two stitches. Count your stitches: You should have 24 stitches. If you don't have 24 stitches, examine your swatch to see if you have increased in each specified stitch. Rework the row if necessary.

Increases in half double, double and treble crochet are shown in Figures 57a, 57b and 57c.

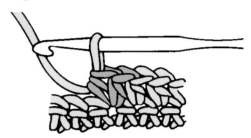

Figure 57a
half double crochet increase

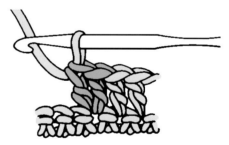

Figure 57b
double crochet increase

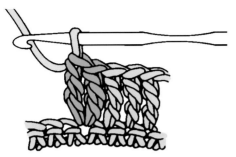

Figure 57c
treble crochet increase

Tip: Make another practice sample by chaining 15 loosely and working four rows of single crochet. Do not fasten off at end of last row. Use this sample swatch to practice the following methods of decreasing stitches.

Decreasing

This is how to work a decrease in the four main stitches. Each decrease gives one fewer stitch than you had before.

Single crochet decrease (sc dec): Insert hook and draw up a loop in each of the next two stitches (three loops now on hook), hook yarn and draw through all three loops on the hook (Figure 58).

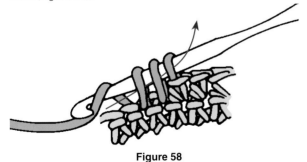

Figure 58

Single crochet decrease made (Figure 59).

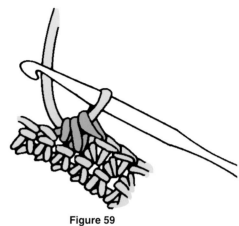

Figure 59

Double crochet decrease (dc dec): Work a double crochet in the specified stitch until two loops remain on the hook (Figure 60).

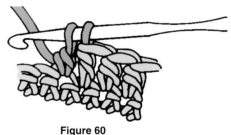

Figure 60

Keeping these two loops on hook, work another double crochet in the next stitch until three loops remain on hook; hook yarn and draw through all three loops on the hook (Figure 61).

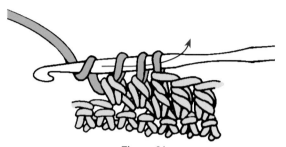

Figure 61

Double crochet decrease made (Figure 62).

Figure 62

Half double crochet decrease (hdc dec): Yo, insert hook in specified stitch and draw up a loop: three loops on the hook (Figure 63).

Figure 63

Keeping these three loops on hook, yo and draw up a loop in the next stitch (five loops now on hook), hook yarn and draw through all five loops on the hook (Figure 64).

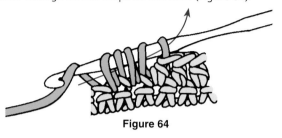

Figure 64

Half double crochet decrease made (Figure 65).

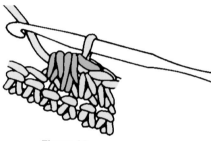

Figure 65

Treble crochet decrease (tr dec): Work a treble crochet in the specified stitch until two loops remain on the hook (Figure 66).

Figure 66

Keeping these two loops on hook, work another treble crochet in the next stitch until three loops remain on the hook; hook yarn and draw through all three loops on the hook (Figure 67).

Treble crochet decrease made (Figure 68).

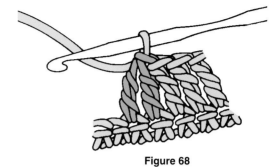

Figure 68

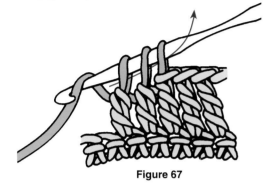

Figure 67

Lesson 11: Joining New Yarn

Never tie or leave knots! In crochet, yarn ends can be easily worked in and hidden because of the density of the stitches. Always leave at least 6 inches when fastening off yarn just used and when joining new yarn. If a flaw or a knot appears in the yarn while you are working from a skein or ball of yarn, cut out the imperfection and rejoin the yarn.

Whenever possible, join new yarn at the end of a row. To do this, work the last stitch with the old yarn until two loops remain on the hook, and then with the new yarn complete the stitch (Figure 69).

To join new yarn in the middle of a row, when about 12 inches of the old yarn remains, work several more stitches with the old yarn, working the stitches over the end of new yarn (Figure 70 shown in double crochet). Then change yarns in the next stitch as previously explained.

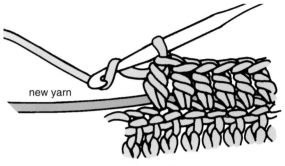

new yarn

Figure 70

Continuing with the new yarn, work the stitches that follow over the old yarn end.

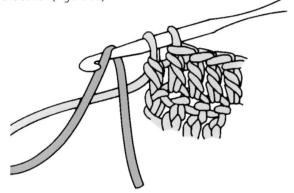

Figure 69

Lesson 12: Finishing & Edging

Finishing

A carefully crocheted project can be disappointing if the finishing is done incorrectly. Correct finishing techniques are not difficult, but they do require time, attention and knowledge of basic techniques.

Weaving in Ends

The first procedure of finishing is to securely weave in all yarn ends. Thread a size 16 steel tapestry needle with yarn end, and then weave running stitches either horizontally or vertically on the wrong side of work. First weave about 1 inch in one direction and then ½ inch in the reverse direction. Be sure yarn doesn't show on the right side of work. Cut off excess yarn. Never weave in more than one yarn end at a time.

Sewing Seams

In order to avoid bulk, edges in crochet are usually butted together for seaming instead of layered. Do not sew too tightly—seams should be elastic and have the same stretch as the crocheted pieces.

Carefully matching stitches and rows as much as possible, sew the seams with the same yarn you used when crocheting.

Invisible seam: This seam provides a smooth, neat appearance because the edges are woven together invisibly from the right side. Join vertical edges, such as side or sleeve seams, through the matching edge stitches, bringing the yarn up through the posts of the stitches (Figure 71).

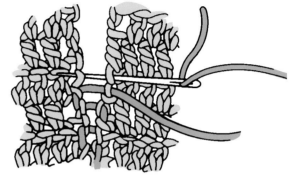

Figure 71

If a firmer seam is desired, weave the edges together through both the tops and the posts of the matching edge stitches.

Backstitch seam: This method gives a strong, firm edge and is used when the seam will have a lot of stress or pull on it. Hold the pieces with right sides together and then sew through both thicknesses as shown (Figure 72).

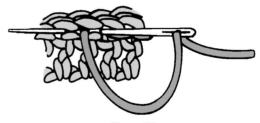

Figure 72

Overcast seam: Strips and pieces of afghans are frequently joined in this manner. Hold the pieces with right sides together and overcast edges, carefully matching stitches on the two pieces (Figure 73).

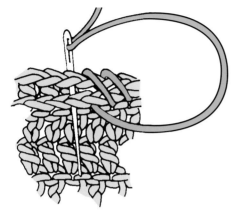

Figure 73

Edges can also be joined in this manner, using only the back loops or the front loops of each stitch (see Stitch Guide on page 126).

Crocheted seam: Holding pieces with right sides together, join yarn with a slip stitch at right-side edge. Loosely slip stitch pieces together, being sure not to pull stitches too tightly (Figure 74). You may wish to use a hook one size larger than the one used in the project.

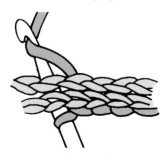

Figure 74

Edging

Single Crochet Edging

A row of single crochet worked around a completed project gives a finished look. The instructions will say to "work a row of single crochet, taking care to keep work flat." This means you need to adjust your stitches as you work. To work the edging, insert hook from front to back through the edge stitch and work a single crochet. Continue evenly along the edge. You may need to skip a row or a stitch here or there to keep the edging from rippling, or add a stitch to keep the work from pulling.

When working around a corner, it is usually necessary to work at least three stitches in the corner centre stitch to keep the corner flat and square (Figure 75).

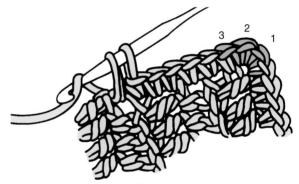

Figure 75

Reverse Single Crochet Edging

A single crochet edging is sometimes worked from left to right for a more dominant edge. To work reverse single crochet, insert hook in stitch to the right (Figure 76), hook yarn and draw through stitch, hook yarn and draw through both loops on the hook (Figure 77).

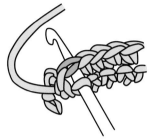

Figure 76

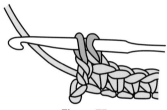

Figure 77

Decorative Edging

Most decorative edgings begin by working in **back bar of chain** (*illustration below*) for a smoother bottom edge.

Back Bar of Chain

KNIT-LOOK DISHCLOTH

This knit-look dishcloth with simple trim can be thrown in the wash and used time and time again!

Design | Belinda Carter

Skill Level

INTERMEDIATE

Finished Size
8 inches square

Materials
DK weight yarn (3½ oz/215 yds per skein):
    1 skein beige
Size H/8/5mm crochet hook or size needed
    to obtain gauge

Gauge
8 sts = 2 inches; 12 rows = 2 inches

Special Stitches
Back slip stitch (back sl st): Bring yarn to front of work, insert hook as indicated from back to front so hook is facing down (yarn should be to right of hook), move yarn to left going over hook, and then move yarn to right going under hook, thereby catching yarn in hook, pull yarn through st and lp on hook, turning hook counterclockwise so hook is now facing up.

Under back slip stitch (under back sl st): Bring yarn to front of work, insert hook as indicated from back to front so hook is facing down (yarn should be to right of hook), move yarn to left going under hook catching yarn in hook, pull yarn through st and lp on hook, turning hook counterclockwise so hook is now facing up.

Dishcloth

Background
Row 1 (RS): Ch 31, **back sl st** *(see Special Stitches)* in **back bar** *(see illustration on page 45)* of 2nd ch from hook and in back bar of each ch across, turn. *(31 back sl sts)*

Row 2: Ch 1, back sl st in **back lp** *(see Stitch Guide on page 126)* of each st across, turn.

Rows 3–8: Rep row 2.

Row 9: Ch 1, back sl st in back lps of each of first 5 sts, [sl st in back lps of each of next 4 sts, **under back sl st** *(see Special Stitches)* in back lps of each of next 4 sts] twice, sl st in back lps of each of next 4 sts, back sl st in back lps of each of last 5 sts, turn.

Row 10: Ch 1, back sl st in back lps of each of first 5 sts, [under back sl st in **front lps** *(see Stitch Guide on page 126)* of each of next 4 sts, sl st in back lps of each of next 4 sts] twice, under back sl st in front lps of each of next 4 sts, back sl st in each of last 5 sts, turn.

Row 11: Ch 1, back sl st in back lp of each of first 5 sts, [sl st in back lp of each of next 4 sts, under back sl st in front lp of each of next 4 sts] twice, sl st in back lp of each of next 4 sts, back sl st in each of last 5 sts, turn.

Rows 12 and 13: Rep rows 10 and 11.

Row 14: Rep row 10.

Knit-Look Dishcloth
Sample project was crocheted with Cotton Fleece (80 per cent pima cotton/20 per cent merino wool) from Brown Sheep Co.

Row 15: Ch 1, back sl st in back lps of each of first 5 sts, [under back sl st in back lp of each of next 4 sts, sl st in front lp of each of next 4 sts] twice, under back sl st in back lp of each of next 4 sts, back sl st in each of last 5 sts, turn.

Row 16: Rep row 11.

Rows 17–20: [Rep rows 10 and 11 alternately] twice.

Row 21: Ch 1, back sl st in back lp of each of first 5 sts, [sl st in front lp of each of next 4 sts, under back sl st in back lp of each of next 4 sts] twice, sl st in front lp of each of next 4 sts, back sl st in each of last 5 sts, turn.

Rows 22–33: Rep rows 10–21.

Rows 34–38: Rep rows 10–14.

Row 39: Ch 1, back sl st in back lp of each of first 9 sts, [back sl st in front lps of each of next 4 sts, back sl st in back lp of each of next 4 sts] twice, back sl st in back lp of each of last 5 sts, turn.

Rows 40–46: Rep row 2.

Last rnd: Now working in rnds around entire outer edge, [evenly sp 30 sl sts across side, ch 1 *(corner)*] 4 times, join with sl st in beg sl st. Fasten off. ■

TWISTED RIB

Notes

Leave stitches behind post stitches unworked.

Post stitches are worked around post of indicated stitch 2 rows below throughout.

Special Stitch

Front post double treble cross-stitch (fpdtr cross-st):
Sk next 2 sts 2 rows below, **fpdtr** *(see Stitch Guide on page 126)* around post of next st, sc in next st, working in front of post st just made, fpdtr around first sk st 2 rows below.

Background

Row 1 (RS): Ch a multiple of 4 plus 2, sc in **back bar** *(see illustration on page 45)* of 2nd ch from hook, and in back bar of each ch across, turn.

Row 2: Ch 1, sc in each st across, turn.

Row 3: Ch 1, sc in first st, [**fpdtr cross-st** *(see Special Stitch)*, sc in next st] across, turn.

Next rows: Rep rows 2 and 3 to desired length. At end of last row, fasten off. ∎

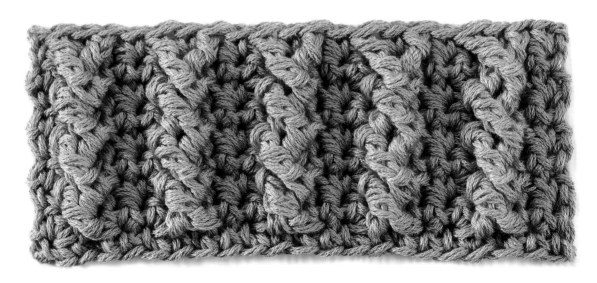

STACKED CLUSTERS

Special Stitch

Cluster (cl): Holding back last lp of each st on hook, 3 dc as indicated, yo, pull through all lps on hook.

Background

Row 1 (RS): Ch a multiple of 3 plus 1 (minimum of 6 plus 1), sc in **back bar** *(see illustration on page 45)* of 2nd ch from hook and in back bar of each ch across, turn.

Row 2: Ch 1, sc in first st, *cl *(see Special Stitch)* in next st**, sc in each of next 2 sts, rep from * across, ending last rep at **, sc in last st, turn.

Row 3: Ch 1, sc in first st, *sl st in next st**, sc in each of next 2 sts, rep from * across, ending last rep at **, sc in last st, turn.

Next rows: Rep rows 2 and 3 to desired length, ending last rep with row 2. At end of last row, fasten off. ■

REVERSE SINGLE CROCHET RIB

Background

Row 1 (RS): Ch any number of chs plus 1 (minimum of 2 plus 1), sc in **back bar** *(see illustration on page 45)* of 2nd ch from hook and in back bar of each ch across, **do not turn**.

Row 2: Work from left to right in **front lps** *(see Stitch Guide on page 126)*, **reverse sc** *(see illustration)* in each st across, do not turn.

Row 3: Working in **back lps** *(see Stitch Guide on page 126)*, sc in each st across, do not turn.

Next rows: Rep rows 2 and 3 alternately to desired length. At end of last row, fasten off. ■

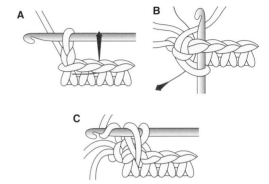

Reverse Single Crochet

SPIKE STITCH RIB

Background

Row 1 (RS): Ch an odd number of chs plus 1 (minimum of 3 plus 1), sc in **back bar** *(see illustration on page 45)* of 2nd ch from hook and in back bar of each ch across, turn.

Row 2: Ch 1, sc in each st across, turn.

Row 3: Ch 1, sc in first st, *insert hook in next st 2 rows below, yo, pull lp through and up even with this row, yo, pull through both lps on hook, sc in next st, rep from * across, turn.

Next rows: Rep rows 2 and 3 to desired length. At end of last row, fasten off. ■

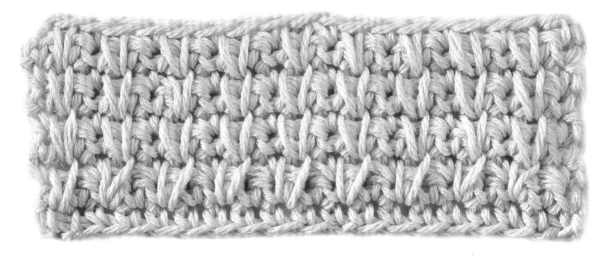

STACKED RIB

Notes

Leave stitches behind post stitches unworked.

Post stitches are worked around post of indicated stitch 2 rows below throughout.

Background

Row 1 (RS): Ch an odd number of chs plus 1 (minimum of 5 plus 1), sc in **back bar** *(see illustration on page 45)* of 2nd ch from hook, and in back bar of each ch across, turn.

Row 2: Ch 1, sc in each st across, turn.

Row 3: Ch 1, sc in first st, *fptr *(see Stitch Guide on page 126)* around post of next st**, sc in next st, rep from * across to last st, ending last rep at **, sc in last st, turn.

Rows 4 and 5: Rep row 2.

Row 6: Ch 1, **bptr** *(see Stitch Guide on page 126)* around post of first st, sc in next st, *bptr around post of next st, sc in next st**, sc in next st, rep from * across to last st, ending last rep at **, sc in last st, turn.

Row 7: Rep row 2.

Next rows: Rep rows 2–7 consecutively to desired length, ending with row 3 or row 6. At end of last row, fasten off. ■

KNITTED RIB

Background

Row 1 (RS): Ch any number of chs plus 1 (minimum of 2 plus 1), sc in **back bar** *(see illustration on page 45)* of 2nd ch from hook and in back bar of each ch across, turn.

Row 2: Ch 2 *(counts as first hdc)*, **hdc in back lp** *(see Stitch Guide on page 126)* of each st across to last st, hdc in back lp of last st, hdc in both lps of same st, turn.

Row 3: Ch 1, sc in back lp of each st across to last 2 sts, sk next st, sc in last st, turn.

Row 4: Rep row 2.

Row 5: Ch 1, sc in **front bar** *(see illustration)* of each st across to last 2 sts, sk next st, sc in last st, turn.

Front Bar of Half Double Crochet

Next rows: Rep rows 2–5 consecutively to desired length. At end of last row, fasten off. ■

BUTTERFLY RIB

Background

Row 1 (RS): Ch 10, sc in **back bar** *(see illustration on page 45)* of 2nd ch from hook, ch 11, sk next 7 chs, sc in back bar of last ch, turn.

Row 2: Ch 1, sc in first st, working in sk chs of row 1, dc in back bar of each of next 7 chs, sc in last st, turn.

Row 3: Ch 1, sc in first st, ch 9, sk next 7 dc, sc in last st, turn.

Row 4: Ch 1, sc in first st, working in sk sts, dc in each of next 7 dc, sc in last st, turn.

Rows 5 and 6: Rep rows 3 and 4.

Row 7: Ch 1, sc in first st, ch 5, holding all chs tog, sc around centre of all chs, ch 5, sk next 7 dc, sc in last st, turn.

Row 8: Rep row 4.

Row 9: Ch 1, sc in first st, ch 11, sk next 7 sts, sc in last st, turn.

Row 10: Rep row 4.

Next rows: Rep rows 3–10 consecutively to desired length, ending with row 8. At end of last row, fasten off. ■

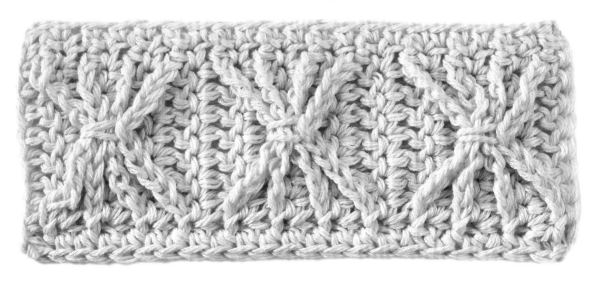

BACK SLIP STITCH RIB

Special Stitch

Back slip stitch (back sl st): Bring yarn to front of work, insert hook as indicated from back to front so hook is facing down *(yarn should be to right of hook)*, move yarn to left going over hook, and then move yarn to right going under hook, thereby catching yarn in hook, pull yarn through st and lp on hook, turning hook counterclockwise so hook is now facing up.

Background

Row 1 (RS): Ch any number of chs (minimum of 3), **back sl st** *(see Special Stitch)* in **back bar** *(see illustration on page 45)* of 2nd ch from hook and in back bar of each ch across, turn.

Row 2: Ch 1, back sl st in **back lp** *(see Stitch Guide on page 126)* of each st across, turn.

Next rows: Rep row 2 to length desired. At end of last row, fasten off. ∎

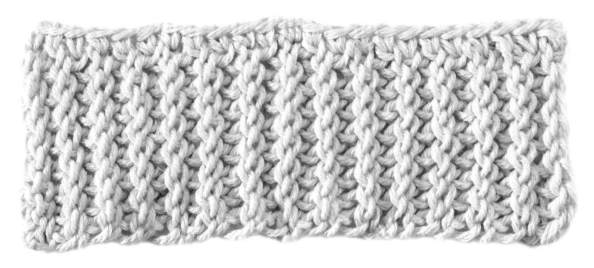

SHOELACE RIB

Notes

Leave stitch behind each post-stitch group unworked.

Post stitches are worked around post of indicated stitch 2 rows below throughout.

Special Stitches

Front post treble crochet group (fptr group): Yo twice, insert hook around post of next st, yo, pull lp through, [yo, pull through 2 lps on hook] twice *(mark this st)*, sk next 3 sts 2 rows below, yo 4 times, insert hook around post of next st, yo, pull lp through, [yo, pull through 2 lps on hook] 4 times, yo, pull through all lps on hook.

Opposite front post treble crochet group (opposite fptr group): Yo 4 times, insert hook around post of marked st, yo, pull lp through, [yo, pull through 2 lps on hook] 4 times, yo twice, insert hook around post of same st as 2nd st of previous fptr group, yo, pull lp through, [yo, pull through 2 lps on hook] twice, yo, pull through all lps on hook.

Background

Row 1 (RS): Ch a multiple of 7 plus 1 (minimum of 14 plus 1), sc in **back bar** *(see illustration on page 45)* of 2nd ch from hook and in back bar of each ch across, turn.

Row 2: Ch 1, sc in each st across, turn.

Row 3: Ch 1, sc in first st, *fptr group *(see Special Stitches)*, sc in each of next 3 sts on current row, working in front of previous fptr group, **opposite fptr group** *(see Special Stitches)***, sc in each of next 2 sts on current row, rep from * across to last st, ending last rep at **, sc in last st on current row, turn.

Row 4: Rep row 2.

Row 5: Ch 1, sc in first st, *fptr *(see Stitch Guide on page 126)* around post of next fptr group, sc in each of next 3 sts, fptr around post of next opposite fptr group**, sc in each of next 2 sts, rep from * across, ending last rep at **, sc in last st, turn.

Row 6: Rep row 2.

Row 7: Ch 1, sc in first st, *fptr group, sc in each of next 3 sts on current row, working behind previous fptr group, opposite fptr group**, sc in each of next 2 sts on current row, rep from * across to last st, ending last rep at **, sc in last st on current row, turn.

Rows 8 and 9: Rep rows 4 and 5.

Next rows: Rep rows 2–9 consecutively to desired length, ending with row 3 or row 6. At end of last row, fasten off. ■

CHAIN STITCH RIB

Background

Row 1 (RS): Ch a multiple of 3 plus 3, sc in **back bar** *(see illustration on page 45)* of 2nd ch from hook, [ch 3, sc in back bar of each of next 3 chs] across to last ch, ch 3, sc in back bar of last ch, turn.

Row 2: Ch 1, sk all ch-3 sps, sc in each st across, push all ch-3 sps to front, turn.

Row 3: Ch 1, sc in first st, [ch 3, sc in each of next 3 sts] across to last st, ch 3, sc in last st, turn.

Next rows: Rep rows 2 and 3 alternately to desired length, ending with row 2. At end of last row, fasten off. ■

UP & DOWN RIB

Notes

Leave stitches behind post stitches unworked.

Post stitches are worked around post of indicated stitch 2 rows below throughout.

Special Stitch

Split cluster (split cl): Holding back last lp of each st on hook, fptr around post of st 1 st to right, fptr around post of st 1 st to left, yo, pull through all lps on hook.

Background

Row 1 (RS): Ch a multiple of 8 plus 2, sc in **back bar** *(see illustration on page 45)* of 2nd ch from hook and in back bar of each ch across, turn.

Row 2: Ch 1, sc in each st across, turn.

Row 3: Ch 1, sc in first st, *sk next st 2 rows below, **fptr** *(see Stitch Guide on page 126)* around post of next st, sc in next st, fptr around post of same st as last post st, sc in each of next 2 sts on current row, **split cl** *(see Special Stitch)*, sc in each of next 2 sts on current row, rep from * across, turn.

Next rows: Rep rows 2 and 3 alternately to desired length. At end of last row, fasten off. ■

LADDER RIB

Notes

Leave stitches behind post stitches unworked.

Post stitches are worked around post of indicated stitch 2 rows below throughout.

Special Stitch

Rung cluster (rung cl): Holding back last lp of each st on hook, **fpdtr** *(see Stitch Guide on page 126)* around post of last post st made, fptr around next st, yo, pull through all lps on hook.

Background

Row 1 (RS): Ch multiple of 7 plus 1 (minimum of 14 plus 1), sc in **back bar** *(see illustration on page 45)* of 2nd ch from hook and in back bar of each ch across, turn.

Row 2: Ch 1, sc in each st across, turn.

Row 3: Ch 1, sc in first st, *fptr *(see Stitch Guide on page 126)* around post of next st, sc in each of next 3 sts, **rung cl**** *(see Special Stitch)*, sc in each of next 2 sts, rep from * across, ending last rep at **, sc in last st, turn.

Next rows: Rep rows 2 and 3 to 1 row less than desired length, ending last rep with row 2.

Last row: Ch 1, sc in first st, *fptr around post of next st, sc in each of next 3 sts, fptr around post of next st**, sc in each of next 2 sts, rep from * across, ending last rep at **, sc in last st. Fasten off. ∎

TWISTED CABLE RIB

Notes

Leave stitches behind post stitches unworked.

Post stitches are worked around post of indicated stitch 2 rows below throughout.

Special Stitch

Front post triple treble crochet (fptrtr): Yo 4 times, insert hook around post of next st, yo, pull lp through, [yo, pull through 2 lps on hook] 5 times.

Background

Row 1 (RS): Ch a multiple of 7 plus 1 (minimum of 14 plus 1), sc in **back bar** *(see illustration on page 45)* of 2nd ch from hook and in back bar of each ch across, turn.

Row 2: Ch 1, sc in each st across, turn.

Row 3: Ch 1, sc in first st, sk next 3 sts 2 rows below, ***fptrtr** (see Special Stitch)* around post of each of next 2 sts, sc in next st on current row, working in front of fptr just made, fptrtr around post of first sk st, fptrtr around post of next sk st**, sc in each of next 2 sts on current row, sk next 5 sts 2 rows below, rep from * across, ending last rep at **, sc in last st, turn.

Next rows: Rep rows 2 and 3 to desired length. At end of last row, fasten off. ■

SLANTED RIB

Notes

Leave stitches behind post stitches unworked.

Post stitches are worked around post of indicated stitch 2 rows below throughout.

Background

Row 1 (RS): Ch a multiple of 7 plus 1 (minimum of 15), sc in **back bar** *(see illustration on page 45)* of 2nd ch from hook and in back bar of each ch across, turn.

Row 2: Ch 1, sc in each st across, turn.

Row 3: Ch 1, sc in first st, sk first 3 sts 2 rows below, *fpdtr *(see Stitch Guide on page 126)* around post of next

st, sc next st on current row, sk next st 2 rows below, fpdtr around post of next st**, sc in each of next 4 sts on current row, sk next 4 sts 2 rows below, rep from * across, ending last rep at **, sc in each rem st across, turn.

Row 4: Rep row 2.

Row 5: Ch 1, sc in first st, sk first 3 sts 2 rows below, *fpdtr around next fpdtr, sc next st on current row, fpdtr around next st**, sc in each of next 4 sts on current row, sk next 6 sts 2 rows below, rep from * across, ending last rep at **, sc in each rem st across, turn.

Next rows: Rep rows 4 and 5 alternately to desired length. At end of last row, fasten off. ■

DOUBLE CABLES RIB

Notes
Leave stitches behind post stitches unworked.

Post stitches are worked around post of indicated stitch 2 rows below throughout.

Special Stitch
Front post triple treble crochet (fptrtr): Yo 4 times, insert hook around post of next st, yo, pull lp through, [yo, pull through 2 lps on hook] 5 times.

Background
Row 1 (RS): Ch a multiple of 6 chs plus 2 (minimum of 12 plus 2), sc in **back bar** *(see illustration on page 45)* of 2nd ch from hook and in back bar of each ch across, turn.

Row 2: Ch 1, sc in each st across, turn.

Row 3: Ch 1, sc in first st, *fptr *(see Stitch Guide on page 126)* around post of each of next 2 sts**, sc in next st, rep from * across, ending last rep at **, sc in last st, turn.

Row 4: Rep row 2.

Row 5: Ch 1, sc in first st, *sk next 3 sts 2 rows below, **fptrtr** *(see Special Stitch)* around post of each of next 2 sts, sc in next st, working in front of last post st, fptrtr around post of first sk st, fptrtr around next sk st**, sc in next st, rep from * across, ending last rep at **, sc in last st, turn.

Next rows: Rep rows 2–5 consecutively to desired length. At end of last row, fasten off. ■

HALF DOUBLE CROCHET RIB

Background

Row 1 (RS): Ch a multiple of 4 plus 1 (minimum of 8 plus 1), hdc in **back bar** *(see illustration on page 45)* of 3rd ch from hook and in back bar of each ch across, turn.

Row 2: Ch 2 *(counts as first hdc)*, *hdc in **back lp** *(see Stitch Guide on page 126)* of each of next 2 sts**, hdc in **front lp** *(see Stitch Guide on page 126)* of each of next 2 sts, rep from * across, ending last rep at **, hdc in both lps of last st, turn.

Row 3: Ch 2, *hdc in back lp of each of next 2 sts**, hdc in front lp of each of next 2 sts, rep from * across, ending last rep at **, hdc in both lps of last st, turn.

Next rows: Rep rows 2 and 3 to desired length. At end of last row, fasten off. ■

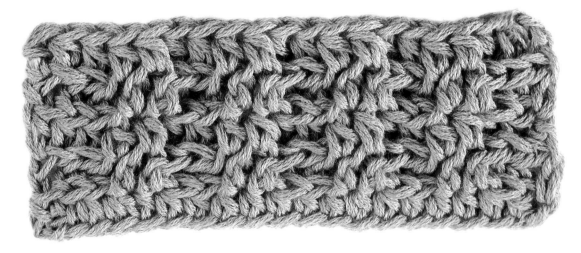

ZIGZAG RIB

Notes

Leave stitches behind post stitches unworked.

Post stitches are worked around post of indicated stitch 2 rows below throughout.

Background

Row 1 (RS): Ch a multiple of 9 chs plus 1, sc in **back bar** *(see illustration on page 45)* of 2nd ch from hook and in back bar of each ch across, turn.

Row 2: Ch 1, sc in each st across, turn.

Row 3: Ch 1, sc in first st, sk next 3 sts 2 rows below, **fpdtr** *(see Stitch Guide on page 126)* around post of next st, *sc in each of next 2 sts on current row, sk next 2 sts 2 rows below, fpdtr around post of next st, rep from * across to last 2 sts, sc in each of last 2 sts, turn.

Row 4: Rep row 2.

Row 5: Ch 1, sc in each of first 4 sts, *fpdtr around post of next st 3 sts to right**, sc in each of next 2 sts, rep from * across, ending last rep at **, sc in last st, turn.

Next rows: Rep rows 2–5 consecutively to desired length. At end of last row, fasten off. ■

POST STITCH RIB

Background

Row 1 (RS): Ch any number of chs plus 2 (minimum of 3 plus 2), dc in **back bar** *(see illustration on page 45)* of 4th ch from hook and in back bar of each ch across, **do not turn.**

Row 2: Ch 2, **fpdc** *(see Stitch Guide on page 126)* around post of each st across to last st, hdc in last st, turn.

Next rows: Rep row 2 to desired length. At end of last row, fasten off. ■

SINGLE CROCHET RIB

Notes

Change colour in last stitch made.

Carry colour not in use up side of work.

Background

Row 1 (RS): With MC, ch any number of chs plus 1 (minimum of 2 plus 1), sc in **back bar** *(see illustration on page 45)* of 2nd ch from hook and in back bar of each rem ch across, **changing colours** *(see Stitch Guide on page 126 and Notes)* to CC, turn.

Row 2: Working in **back lps** *(see Stitch Guide on page 126)*, ch 1, sc in each st across, turn.

Row 3: Working in back lps, ch 1, sc in each st across, changing to MC, turn.

Row 4: Rep row 2.

Row 5: Rep row 3, changing to CC.

Next rows: Rep rows 2–5 to 1 row less than desired length, ending with row 4. At end of last row, fasten off CC.

Last row: With MC, rep row 2, **do not turn**.

End row: Working in ends of rows, ch 1, sc in end of each row across. Fasten off. ■

PONCHO DOLL FRINGE SCARF

The poncho doll fringe on this scarf creates a fun look and will be quite the conversation piece!

Design | Belinda Carter

Skill Level

INTERMEDIATE

Finished Size

5 x 55 inches, including fringe

Materials

DK weight yarn (3½ oz/215 yds):
- 2 skeins light orange (MC)
- 1 skein beige (CC)

Size H/8/5mm crochet hook or size needed to obtain gauge

Cardboard:
- 4-inch piece
- 3½-inch piece

Gauge

18 sts = 5 inches; 10 rows = 3 inches

Notes

Leave stitches behind post stitches unworked.

Post stitches are worked around post of indicated stitch 2 rows below throughout.

Special Stitch

Close single crochet (close sc): Insert hook in **back lp** *(see Stitch Guide on page 126)* of sk st 2 rows below, and then insert hook in st 1 row below this row, yo, pull through st and back lp, yo, pull through all lps on hook.

Scarf

Row 1: With MC, ch 19, sc in **back bar** *(see illustration on page 45)* of 2nd ch from hook and in back bar of each ch across, turn.

Row 2: Ch 1, sc in each st across, turn.

Row 3: Ch 1, sc in first st, *fptr *(see Stitch Guide on page 126)* around post of next st, sc in next st, sk next 2 sts 2 rows below, **fpdtr** *(see Stitch Guide on page 126)* around next st, sc in next st, working in front of last post st, fpdtr around first sk st, sc in next st, fptr around next st*, sc in each of next 2 sts, rep between *, sc in last st, turn.

Poncho Doll Fringe Scarf
Sample project was crocheted with Cotton
Fleece (80 per cent pima cotton/20 per
cent merino wool) from Brown Sheep Co.

Row 4: Rep row 2.

Row 5: Ch 1, sc in first st, *[sk next 2 sts 2 rows below, fpdtr around next st, sc in next st, working in back of last post st, fpdtr in first sk st, sc in next st] twice*, sc in next st, rep between *, turn.

Row 6: Rep row 2.

Row 7: Ch 1, sc in first st, fptr around next st, sc in next st, *sk next 2 sts 2 rows below, fpdtr around next st, sc in next st, working in front of last post st, fpdtr around first sk st*, sc in each of next 2 sts, fptr around next st to right, fptr around st 1 st to left, sc in each of next 2 sc, rep between * once, sc in next st, fptr around next st, sc in last st, turn.

Row 8: Ch 1, sc in each of first 8 sts, **close sc** *(see Special Stitch, page 68)* in each of next 2 sts, sc in each of last 8 sts, turn.

Row 9: Ch 1, sc in first st, *sk next 2 sts 2 rows below, fpdtr around next st, sc in next st, working in back of last post st, fpdtr around first sk st, sc in next st*, fptr around next st, sc in each of next 2 sts, sk next st 2 rows below, fptr around next st, working in front of last post st, fptr around sk st, sc in each of next 2 sts, fptr around next st, sc in next st, rep between * once, turn.

Row 10: Rep row 8.

Row 11: Ch 1, sc in first st, fptr around next st, sc in next st, *sk next 2 sts 2 rows below, fpdtr around next st, sc in next st, working in front of last post st, fpdtr around first sk st*, sc in each of next 2 sts, fptr around each of next 2 sts, sc in each of next 2 sts, rep between * once, sc in next st, fptr around next st, sc in last st, turn.

Rows 12 and 13: Rep rows 8 and 9.

Row 14: Rep row 8.

Row 15: Ch 1, sc in first st, fptr around next st, sc in next st, *sk next 2 sts 2 rows below, fpdtr around next st, sc in next st, working in front of last post st, fpdtr around first sk st*, sc in next st, sk next st 2 rows below, fptr around next st, sc in each of next 2 sts, fptr around post st 2 sts to right, sc in next st, rep between * once, sc in next st, fptr around next st, sc in last st, turn.

Row 16: Rep row 2.

Row 17: Rep row 5.

Next rows: Rep rows 2–17 consecutively until piece measures 49 inches from beg, ending last rep with row 3. At end of last row, fasten off.

Poncho Doll Fringe
Make 4

Doll Body
Wrap CC around 4-inch piece of cardboard 30 times.

For **hanger**, cut strand of CC 10 inches long, slide Body off cardboard, insert strand through 1 end of Body lps and tie securely, leaving long ends. Cut lps open at other end.

Doll Head
Cut another strand of CC 6 inches long, wrap around Body ¾ inch from top.

Doll Arms
Wrap CC around 3½-inch piece of cardboard 10 times. Slide Arms off cardboard.

Divide Body in half for front and back, slide Arms between the 2 layers. Cut 10-inch strand of CC and tie around Body just below Arms to form waist.

Trim Body length to 3 inches. Cut ends of lps on Arms. Trim Arms to 2½ inches across.

Cut 2 strands of CC each 6 inches long. Tie 6-inch strands around ends of Arms for hands.

Doll Poncho

Row 1: With MC, ch 2, sc in back bar of 2nd ch from hook, turn.

Row 2: Ch 1, sc in st, turn.

Rows 3–5: Rep row 2.

Row 6: Ch 1, sc in st, **do not turn**.

Row 7: Ch 1, sc in left side of last sc, turn.

Rows 8–12: Rep row 2. At end of last row, fasten off.

Sew end of row 1 to end of row 12.

Finishing

Cut 2½-inch strand of MC for each Fringe on Doll Poncho. Fold strand in half, pull fold through, pull ends through fold. Pull to tighten. Evenly sp Fringe around Poncho.

Place 1 Poncho on each Doll.

Attach 2 Dolls to each end of Scarf as shown in photo above. *Note: You can also place these Poncho Dolls on a band to add this fun fringe to a jacket or a household item as shown in photo below.* ■

KNOTTED FRINGE

Top Band

Row 1 (RS): Ch a multiple of 3 plus 2, sc in **back bar** *(see illustration on page 45)* of 2nd ch from hook and in back bar of each ch across, turn.

Next rows: Work any pattern as desired. At end of last row, fasten off.

Triple-Knot Fringe

Cut strands of yarn twice as long as desired Fringe length plus 3 inches for all knots. Cut 2 strands of yarn for first st on row, and then cut 2 strands of yarn for every 3rd st.

Fold 2 strands of yarn in half with WS of work facing, insert hook in st where Fringe is to be attached, pull fold through st, pull ends through fold. Pull ends to tighten.

Fringe in every 3rd st along bottom edge of Top Band.

First Knots

*Take half the strands of 1 Fringe and half of the strands from the Fringe next to it and tie them tog *(see illustration)* 1 inch from the Top Band. Rep from * across.

2nd Knots

Take the unknotted strands from the first Fringe and half the strands from the next Fringe and tie them tog 1 inch below the last Knot. Continue across Fringe. ■

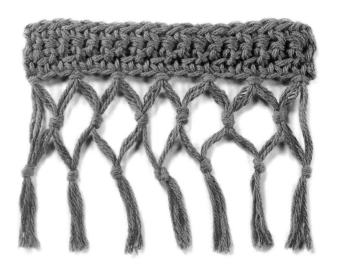

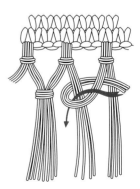

Knotted Fringe

SIDEWAYS CHAINS

Notes

Leave stitches behind post stitches unworked throughout.

Post stitches are worked around post of indicated stitch 2 rows below.

Top Band & Fringe

Row 1 (RS): Ch 15, sl st in **back bar** *(see illustration on page 45)* of 2nd ch from hook, sl st in back bar in each of next 8 chs, sc in back bar of last 5 chs, turn.

Row 2: Ch 1, sc in each of first 5 sts, ch 10, leaving rem sts unworked, turn.

Row 3: Sl st in back bar of 2nd ch from hook and in back bar of each of next 8 chs, sc in next st, [**fptr** *(see*

Stitch Guide on page 126) around post of next st, sc in next st] twice, turn.

Row 4: Rep row 2.

Row 5: Sl st in back bar of 2nd ch from hook, sl st in back bar of each of next 8 chs, sc in next st, sk next 2 sts 2 rows below, **fpdtr** *(see Stitch Guide on page 126)* around post of next st, sc in next st, working in front of last post st, fpdtr around post of first sk st, sc in last st, turn.

Next rows: Rep rows 2–5 consecutively to desired length, ending last rep with row 3 or row 5. At end of last row, fasten off. ∎

FAUX BEADS

Top Band

Row 1: Ch a multiple of 6 plus 1, sc in **back bar** *(see illustration on page 45)* of 2nd ch from hook and in back bar of each ch across, turn.

Row 2: Ch 1, sc in first st, [sc in **front lp** *(see Stitch Guide on page 126)* of next st, sc in **back lp** *(see Stitch Guide on page 126)* of next st] across to last st, sc in both lps of last st, turn.

Row 3: Rep row 2. Fasten off.

Fringe

Cut 1 strand yarn 15 inches long for every 3 sts on Top Band.

Fold strand in half, pull fold through st, pull ends through fold. Pull ends to tighten.

Beg in 2nd st from end, Fringe in every 3rd st across.

Beads

Note: Make 3 beads of various colours for each Fringe.

Round

Rnd 1: Ch 2, 6 sc in 2nd ch from hook, **do not join**. *(6 sc)*

Rnd 2: 2 sc in each st around, join with sl st in beg sc. Leaving long end, fasten off.

Weave long end through sts on last rnd, stuff with a little piece of same-coloured yarn, pull tight to close. Secure end.

Flat

Rnd 1: Ch 2, 8 sc in 2nd ch from hook, **do not join**. Pull end to tighten. *(8 sc)*

Rnd 2: Sl st in each st around, join with sl st in beg sl st. Fasten off.

Assembly

Tie knot in first Fringe ½ inch from top, *with tapestry needle, thread Bead onto Fringe, slip Bead up to knot, tie another knot just below Bead, [tie knot ½ inch from below last knot, thread Bead on Fringe, tie knot just below bead] twice, rep from * across all Fringe.

Trim ends of Fringe as desired. ■

DANGLING BALL FRINGE

Note
Do not join or turn unless otherwise stated.

Ball
Make 1 Ball for every multiple of 4 sts on Top Band

Rnd 1: Ch 2, 4 sc in 2nd ch from hook, **do not join** *(see Note)*. *(4 sc)*

Rnd 2: 2 sc in each st around. *(8 sc)*

Rnd 3: Sc in each st around.

Rnd 4: Rep rnd 3. Leaving long end, fasten off.

Stuff Ball with small amount of fibrefill. Weave long end through sts on last rnd, pull to close. Secure end.

Top Band
Row 1: Ch a multiple of 4 plus 2, sc in **back bar** *(see illustration on page 45)* of 2nd ch from hook and in back bar of each ch across, turn.

Row 2: Ch 1, sc in each st across, turn.

Row 3: Ch 1, sc in first st, [ch 4, sl st in top of Ball, ch 4, sk next 3 sts on Top Band, sc in next st] across. Fasten off and weave in ends. ■

DANGLING CHAINS

Top Band & Fringe

Row 1 (RS): Ch a multiple of 2 plus 1 (minimum of 4 plus 1), sc in **back bar** *(see illustration on page 45)* of 2nd ch from hook and in back bar of each ch across, turn.

Row 2: Ch 1, sc in first st, [sc in **front lp** *(see Stitch Guide on page 126)* of next st, sc in **back lp** *(see Stitch Guide on page 126)* of next st] across to last st, sc in both lps of last st, turn.

Row 3: Ch 1, sc in first st, [ch 10, sl st in back bar of 2nd ch from hook and in back bar of each ch across, sc in next st] across. Fasten off. ■

CUT LOOPS

Note
Design requires 2½-inch piece of cardboard.

Special Stitch
Loop single crochet (loop sc): Wrap yarn from front to back around cardboard, sc in next st *(this will create a lp in back of work)*, remove lp from cardboard.

Top Band & Fringe
Row 1 (WS): Ch any number of chs plus 1 (minimum of 2 plus 1), **loop sc** *(see Special Stitch)* in 2nd ch from hook and in each ch across, turn.

Row 2: Ch 1, sc in each st across, turn. Fasten off.

Finishing
Cut end of each lp open, or lps can be left uncut if desired. ■

LOVE KNOTS

Top Band & Fringe

Row 1: Ch a multiple of 2 sts plus 1 (minimum of 4 plus 1), sc in **back bar** *(see illustration on page 45)* of 2nd ch from hook and in back bar of each ch across, turn.

Row 2: Ch 1, sc in first st, [sc in **front lp** *(see Stitch Guide on page 126)* of next st, sc in **back lp** *(see Stitch Guide on page 126)* of next st] across to last st, sc in last st, turn.

Row 3: Ch 1, sc in first st, *[pull up 1-inch lp, yo, pull lp through lp, sc in back strand of lp] 3 times, pull up 1-inch lp, yo, pull lp through lp, insert hook in back strand of lp, yo, pull through, insert hook in top of last sc, yo, pull through st and all lps on hook**, sc in each of next 2 sts, rep from * across, ending last rep at **, sc in last st. Fasten off. ∎

PRETTY IN PINK BABY BLANKET

Your little princess will love to wrap up in this ruffle-edged blanket.

Design | Belinda Carter

Skill Level
INTERMEDIATE

Finished Size
34 x 40 inches

Materials
DK weight yarn (3½ oz/215 yds per skein):
   8 skeins pink

Size H/8/5mm crochet hook or size needed to
   obtain gauge

Gauge
19 sts = 6 inches; 16 rows = 5 inches

Notes
Leave stitches behind post stitches unworked.

Post stitches are worked around post of indicated stitch 2 rows below throughout.

Join rounds with slip stitch as indicated unless otherwise stated.

Special Stitch
Puff stitch (puff st): [Insert hook in indicated st, yo, pull lp through, yo] 3 times, pull last yo through all lps on hook.

Blanket

Body
Row 1 (RS): Ch 99, sc in **back bar** *(see illustration on page 45)* of 2nd ch from hook and in back bar of each ch across, turn. *(98 sc)*

Row 2: Ch 1, **puff st** *(see Special Stitch)* in first st, ch 1, sk next st, *[puff st in next st, ch 1, sk next st] 3 times, sc in each of next 10 sts**, puff st in next st, ch 1, sk next st, rep from * across to last 8 sts, ending last rep at **, [puff st in next st, ch 1, sk next st] 3 times, puff st in next st, sc in last st, turn.

Row 3: Ch 1, sc in each of first 9 sts or chs, *[puff st, ch 1, sk next st] 4 times**, sc in each of next 10 sts, rep from * across to last 8 sts, ending last rep at **, sc in each of last 9 sts, turn.

Rows 4–9: [Rep rows 2 and 3 alternately] 3 times.

Row 10: Ch 1, sc in each st across, turn.

Rows 11–117: [Rep rows 2–10 consecutively] 12 times, ending with row 9, which is a RS row. At end of last row, **do not turn**.

Edging

Rnd 1 (RS): With RS facing and working in ends of rows, *evenly sp 117 sc across to corner, ch 2 for corner*, evenly sp 97 sc in starting ch on opposite side of row 1, ch 2 for corner, rep between * once, ch 2 for corner, evenly sp 97 sc across top, ch 2 for corner, **join** *(see Notes)* in beg sc, turn.

Rnd 2: Ch 1, sc in corner ch sp, sc in each st around with (sc, ch 2, sc) in each corner, ending with (sc, ch 2) in same ch sp as first sc, join in beg sc, turn.

Rnd 3: Ch 1, sc in corner ch sp, *[sc in next st, **fptr** *(see Stitch Guide on page 126)* around post of next st] across to last st before ch sp, sc in last st**, (sc, ch 2, sc) in corner ch sp, rep from * around, ending last rep at **, (sc, ch 2) in same ch sp as first sc, join in beg sc, turn.

Rnd 4: Ch 1, sc in corner ch sp, *sc in each of next 2 sts, [3 sc in next st, sc in next st] across to last st before corner, sc in last st**, (sc, ch 2, sc) in corner ch sp, rep from * around, ending last rep at **, (sc, ch 2) in same ch sp as first sc, join in beg sc, turn.

Rnd 5: Ch 1, sc in corner ch sp, *sc in next st, fptr around post of next st, [sc in each of next 2 sts, 3 sc in next st, sc in next st] across to last 3 sts before corner, sc in next st, fptr around post of next st, sc in next st**, (sc, ch 2, sc) in corner ch sp, rep from * around, ending last rep at **, (sc, ch 2) in same ch sp as first sc, join in beg sc, turn.

Rnd 6: Ch 1, sc in corner ch sp, *sc in next st, **bptr** *(see Stitch Guide on page 126)* around post of next st, sc in each of next 2 sts, [ch 1, sk next 5 sts, sc in next st] across to last 3 sts before corner, sc in next st, bptr around post of next st, sc in next st**, (sc, ch 2, sc) in corner ch sp, rep from * around, ending last rep at **, (sc, ch 2) in same ch sp as first sc, join in beg sc. Fasten off. ■

Pretty in Pink Baby Blanket
Sample project was crocheted with Cotton Fleece (80 per cent pima cotton/20 per cent merino wool) from Brown Sheep Co.

TRADITIONAL RUFFLE

Background

Row 1 (RS): Ch 12, sc in **back bar** *(see illustration on page 45)* of 2nd ch from hook, sc in back bar of each of next 2 chs, dc in back bar of each of last 8 chs, turn.

Row 2: Ch 3 *(counts as first dc)*, dc in **front lp** *(see Stitch Guide on page 126)* of each st across to last 3 sts, sc in both lps of next st, dc in both lps of next st, sc in both lps of last st, turn.

Row 3: Ch 1, sc in each of first 3 sts, dc in front lp of each st across to last st, dc in both lps of last st, turn.

Next rows: Rep rows 2 and 3 alternately to desired length, ending last rep with row 2. At end of last row, fasten off. ■

LITTLE FRILLS

Special Stitch

Surface stitch (surface st): Holding yarn at back of work, insert hook between rows, yo, pull lp through st and lp on hook.

Background

Row 1: Ch 8, sc in **back bar** *(see illustration on page 45)* of 2nd ch from hook *(mark this as st #2)*, sc in back bar of next ch *(mark this as st #4)*, sc in back bar of each ch across, turn.

Row 2: Ch 1, sc in each st across, turn.

Next rows: Rep row 2 to desired length, working in multiple of 6 rows plus 1.

Last row: Ch 1, sc in each of first 5 sts, sc in next st *(mark this as st #3)*, sc in last st *(mark this as st #1)*, **do not turn.**

Edging

Working in ends of rows, ch 1, sc in end of each row across. Fasten off.

Surface Stitch Ruffle

Row 1: Surface st *(see Special Stitch)* in st #1, surface st across rows to st #2, surface st in next row, *insert hook from front to back through next row, sk next row, insert hook from back to front through next row, sk next row, insert hook from front to back through next row, yo, pull through all rows and lp on hook, surface st in next row, rep from * across. Fasten off.

Row 2: Using the same procedure as established in row 1, work surface sts from st #3 to st #4. ■

ROWS OF RUFFLES

Background

Row 1 (RS): Ch any number of chs plus 1 (minimum of 2 plus 1), sc in **back bar** *(see illustration on page 45)* of 2nd ch from hook and in back bar of each ch across, turn.

Row 2: Ch 1, sc in each st across, turn.

Row 3: Rep row 2.

Row 4a: Working in **front lps** *(see Stitch Guide on page 126)*, ch 1, sc in each st across, turn.

Row 4b: Working in **back lps** *(see Stitch Guide on page 126)* of row 3, 3 sc in each st across, sl st in beg sc of row 4a.

Row 5 (WS): Ch 1, sc in each st across row 4a, turn.

Row 6a: Working in front lps of row 5, ch 1, sc in each st across, turn.

Row 6b: Working in back lps of row 5, 3 sc in each st across, sl st in beg sc of row 6a, turn.

Row 7 (RS): Ch 1, sc in each st across row 6b, turn.

Rows 8–11: Rep rows 4a–7. At end of last row, fasten off. ■

BOX PLEATS

Background

Row 1 (RS): Ch a multiple of 6 plus 5, sc in **back bar** *(see illustration on page 45)* of 2nd ch from hook and in back bar of each ch across, turn.

Row 2a: Ch 1, sc in **front lp** *(see Stitch Guide on page 126)* of each st on row 1 across, turn.

Row 2b: Ch 1, sc in **back lp** *(see Stitch Guide on page 126)* of each st on row 1 across, turn.

Row 3: Ch 1, sc in first st of row 2a and row 2b *at same time*, sc in next st of row 2a and row 2b *at same time*, *sc in front lp of each of next 3 sts on row 2a, **turn**, working in unworked lps of row 2a and back lps of 2b *at same time*, sc in each of next 3 sts, **turn**, working in rem lps of row 2b, sc in each of next 3 sts, [sc in next st on row 2a and next st on row 2b *at same time*] twice, rep from * across, turn.

Row 4: Ch 1, sc in first st, [sc in front lp of next st, sc in back lp of next st] across to last st, sc in both lps of last st, turn.

Next row: Rep row 4 to desired length. At end of last row, fasten off. ■

BABY BELLS

Notes

Leave stitches behind post stitches unworked.

Post stitches are worked around post of indicated stitch 2 rows below throughout.

Background

Row 1 (RS): Ch an odd number of chs plus 1 (minimum of 5 plus 1), sc in **back bar** *(see illustration on page 45)* of 2nd ch from hook and in back bar of each ch across, turn.

Row 2: Ch 1, sc in each st across, turn.

Row 3: Ch 1, sc in first st, [**fptr** *(see Stitch Guide on page 126)* around post of next st, sc in next st] across, turn.

Row 4: Ch 1, sc in first st, [3 sc in next st, sc in next st] across, turn.

Row 5: Ch 1, sc in each of first 2 sts, *3 sc in next st**, sc in each of next 3 sts, rep from * across, ending last rep at **, sc in each of last 2 sts, turn.

Row 6: Ch 1, sc in first st, [ch 1, sk next 5 sts, sc in next st] across. Fasten off. ■

RIBS & BELLS

Notes

Leave stitches behind post stitches unworked.

Post stitches are worked around post of indicated stitch 1 row below.

Background

Row 1 (WS): Ch a multiple of 6 plus 6, hdc in **back bar** *(see illustration on page 45)* of 3rd ch from hook *(beg 2 sk chs count as first hdc)* and in back bar of each ch across, turn.

Row 2: Ch 2 *(counts as first hdc)*, [**fpdc** *(see Stitch Guide on page 126)* around post of **next st** *(see Notes)*, **bpdc** *(see Stitch Guide on page 126)* around post of next st] across to last 2 sts, fpdc around post of next st, hdc in last st, turn.

Row 3: Ch 2, [bpdc around post of next st, fpdc around post of next st] across to last 2 sts, bpdc around post of next st, hdc in last st, turn.

Row 4: Ch 2, *[fpdc around post of next st, bpdc around post of next st] twice, ch 1, 3 hdc in next st, ch 1, bpdc around post of next st, rep from * across to last 4 sts, fpdc around post of next st, bpdc around post of next st, fpdc around post of next st, hdc in last st, turn.

Row 5: Ch 2, *[bpdc around post of next st, fpdc around post of next st] twice, ch 1, hdc in next ch sp, hdc in each of next 3 sts, hdc in next ch sp, ch 1, fpdc around post of next st, rep from * across to last 4 sts, bpdc around post of next st, fpdc around post of next st, bpdc around post of next st, hdc in last st, turn.

Row 6: Ch 2, *[fpdc around post of next st, bpdc around post of next st] twice, ch 1, hdc in next ch sp, hdc in each of next 5 sts, hdc in next ch sp, ch 1, bpdc around post of next st, rep from * across to last 4 sts, fpdc around post of next st, bpdc around post of next st, fpdc around post of next st, hdc in last st, turn.

Row 7: Ch 2, *[bpdc around post of next st, fpdc around post of next st] twice, ch 1, hdc in next ch sp, hdc in each of next 7 sts, hdc in next ch sp, ch 1, fpdc around post of next st, rep from * across to last 4 sts, bpdc around post of next st, fpdc around post of next st, bpdc around post of next st, hdc in last st. Fasten off. ∎

DOUBLE TROUBLE

Background

Row 1: Ch a multiple of 3 plus 1 (minimum of 6 plus 1), sc in **back bar** *(see illustration on page 45)* of 2nd ch from hook and in back bar of each ch across, turn.

Row 2: Ch 1, sc in each st across, turn.

First Layer Ruffle

Row 1: Ch 1, sc in **front lp** *(see Stitch Guide on page 126)* of first st, *ch 1, (sc, ch 1, sc) in front lp of next st, ch 1**, sc in front lp of each of next 2 sts, rep from * across, ending last rep at **, sc in front lp of last st, turn.

Row 2: Ch 1, sc in first st, *ch 1, sk next ch-1 sp, sc in next sc, ch 1, sc in next ch-1 sp, ch 1, sc in next sc, ch 1, sk next ch-1 sp**, sc in each of next 2 sc, rep from * across, ending last rep at **, sc in last st, turn.

Row 3: Ch 1, sc in first st, *ch 1, sk next ch-1 sp, sc in next sc, ch 1, sc in next ch-1 sp, ch 1, sk next sc, sc in next ch-1 sp, ch 1, sc in next sc, ch 1, sk next ch-1 sp**, sc in each of next 2 sc, rep from * across, ending last rep at **, sc in last st. Fasten off.

2nd Layer Ruffle

Row 1 (RS): With RS facing, join with sc in unworked lp of row 2, sc in each unworked lp across, turn.

Rows 2–4: Ch 1, sc in each st across, turn.

Row 5: Ch 1, sc in first st, *ch 1, (sc, ch 1, sc) in next st, ch 1**, sc in each of next 2 sts, rep from * across, ending last rep at **, sc in last st, turn.

Rows 6 and 7: Rep rows 2 and 3 of First Layer Ruffle. Fasten off. ■

LOOPY LACE

Note
Design requires 2 hooks; 1 should be 1 size larger than the other.

Background
Row 1 (RS): With smaller hook, ch any number of chs plus 1 (minimum of 3 plus 1), sc in **back bar** *(see illustration on page 45)* of 2nd ch from hook and in back bar of each ch across, turn.

Row 2: Ch 1, sc in each st across, turn.

Row 3: Change to larger hook. Rep row 2.

Row 4: Ch 1, sc in first st, [sc in **front lp** *(see Stitch Guide on page 126)* of next st, sc in **back lp** *(see Stitch Guide on page 126)* of same st] across to last st, sc in both lps of last st, turn.

Row 5: Ch 1, sc in first st, [sc in front lp of next st, sc in back lp of next st] across to last st, sc in both lps of last st, turn.

Next rows: Rep row 5 to desired length. At end of last row, fasten off. ∎

POST STITCH RUFFLE

Notes

Leave stitches behind post stitches unworked.

Post stitches are worked around post of indicated stitch 2 rows below throughout.

Background

Row 1 (RS): Ch a multiple of 3 plus 1, sc in **back bar** *(see illustration on page 45)* of 2nd ch from hook and in back bar of each ch across, turn.

Row 2: Ch 1, sc in each st across, turn.

Rows 3 and 4: Rep row 2.

Row 5: Ch 1, sc in first st, ***fpdc** *(see Stitch Guide on page 126)* around post of next st**, sc in each of next 2 sts, rep from * across, ending last rep at **, sc in last st.

Next rows: Rep rows 2–5 consecutively until desired length. At end of last row, fasten off. ■

LACED CHAINS

Background

Row 1 (RS): Ch a multiple of 8 chs plus 6, sc in **back bar** *(see illustration on page 45)* of 2nd ch from hook, and in back bar of each ch across, turn.

Row 2: Ch 1, sc in each st across, turn.

Ruffle

Row 1: Ch 1, sc in first st, ch 5, sk next st, sc in next st, [ch 7, sk next 3 sts, sc in next st] across to last 2 sts, ch 5, sk next st, sc in last st, turn.

Row 2: Ch 1, with ch-5 lp in back of work, sc in first sk st, [ch 7, with ch-7 lp in front of work, sc in centre sk st of next 3 sk sts, ch 7, with ch-7 lp in back of work, sc in centre sk st of next 3 sk sts] across to last 2 sts, ch 5, with ch-5 lp in front of work, sc in last sk st. Fasten off. ■

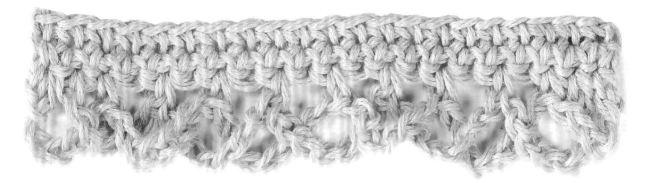

GATHERED RUFFLES

Background

Row 1: Ch 12, sc in **back bar** *(see illustration on page 45)* of 2nd ch from hook, [ch 1, sk next ch, sc in back bar of next ch] across, turn.

Row 2: Ch 1, sc in first st, [ch 1, sk next ch sp, sc in next st] across, turn.

Next rows: Rep row 2 to desired length, ending with an odd-numbered row. At end of last row, fasten off.

Gathering

Turn rows sideways. Using tapestry needle, weave strand of yarn through top horizontal rows of ch-1 sps and then weave through next row of ch-1 sp directly underneath, pull strand to gather up rows, secure ends. ∎

EYELET RUFFLES

Note

This design creates a natural eyelet in row 2 at the front of each ruffle. If desired, push end of crochet hook through each opening on row 2 to open eyelet more fully.

Background

Row 1 (RS): Ch a multiple of 6 plus 3, sc in **back bar** *(see illustration on page 45)* of 2nd ch from hook and in back bar of each ch across, turn.

Row 2: Ch 1, sc in each st across, turn.

Row 3: Rep row 2.

Row 4: Ch 1, sc in each of first 2 sts, [sk next 4 sts, sc in next st, push sk sts to back of work, sc in next st] across to last st, sc in last st, turn.

Row 5 (RS): Ch 1, sc in first st, [sk first sk st 2 rows below, insert hook in **front lp** *(see Stitch Guide on page 126)* of next sk st, *insert hook in both lps of next st 1 row below, yo, pull through st and lp on hook, yo, pull through all lps on hook*, insert hook in front lp of next sk st 2 rows below, rep between * once] across to last st, sc in last st, turn. Fasten off. ■

PEEKABOO RUFFLE

Notes

Leave stitches behind post stitches unworked.

Post stitches are worked around post of indicated stitch 4 rows below throughout.

Background

Row 1 (RS): Ch 10, sc in **back bar** *(see illustration on page 45)* of 2nd ch from hook and in back bar of each ch across, turn.

Row 2: Ch 1, sc in first st, [sc in **front lp** *(see Stitch Guide on page 126)* of next st, sc in **back lp** *(see Stitch Guide on page 126)* of next st] 3 times, sc in front lp of next st, sc in both lps of last st, turn.

Rows 3–5: Rep row 2.

Row 6: Ch 1, sc in first st, [fpdc *(see Stitch Guide on page 126)* around post of next st, sc in next st] across, turn.

Rows 7–11: Rep row 2.

Row 12: Rep row 6.

Next rows: Rep rows 2–12 consecutively to desired length, ending with row 12.

Last row: Rep row 2, **do not turn.**

Edging

Row 1: With RS facing and working in ends of rows, ch 1, sc in end of first row, [ch 2, sk ends of next 5 rows, sc in end of next row *(this row should be between 2 ruffles)*] across, work last sc in end of last row, turn.

Row 2: Ch 1, sc in each sc and in each ch across. Fasten off. ■

PRETTY BITTY BOWS

Background

Row 1: Ch a multiple of 5 plus 1 (minimum of 10 plus 1), sc in **back bar** *(see illustration on page 45)* of 2nd ch from hook, and in back bar of each ch across, turn.

Row 2: Ch 1, sc in each st across, turn.

First Ruffle

Row 1: Ch 1, sc in first st, [ch 3, sc in next st] 4 times, leaving rem sts unworked, turn.

Row 2: Ch 1, sc in first ch-3 sp, [ch 3, sc in next ch-3 sp] 3 times, turn.

Row 3: Ch 1, sc in first ch-3 sp, [ch 3, sc in next ch-3 sp] twice, turn.

Row 4: Ch 1, sc in first ch-3 sp, ch 3, sc in last ch-3 sp. Fasten off.

Next Ruffle

Row 1: Join with sc in next unworked st on row 2 of Background, [ch 3, sc in next st] 4 times, leaving rem sts unworked, turn.

Rows 2–4: Rep rows 2–4 of First Ruffle.

Rep Next Ruffle across until all sts are used.

Bow

Cut 12-inch strands of CC, cutting 1 more strand than number of Ruffles.

Tie strands into bows connecting Ruffles tog through ch-3 sps on row 1 of Ruffles. Tie 1 strand in bow around row 1 at each end of Ruffles. ■

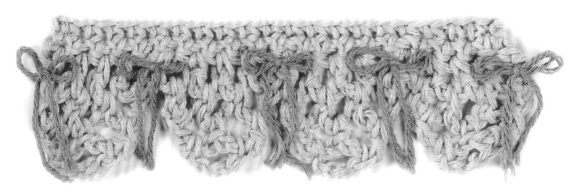

BEADED EDGINGS GENERAL DIRECTIONS

Making beaded crochet trims is not so very different than plain crochet trims. The main difference is that beads are strung onto your crochet cotton before you begin and then moved into place as stitches are formed. There are two main classes of stitches: beaded stitches and reverse beaded stitches. With beaded stitches, the beads naturally pop up on the wrong side of your work. With reverse beaded stitches, the beads come up on the right side.

A beaded stitch is worked exactly like its non-beaded counterpart except that you pull a bead up close to your hook at the appropriate moment and incorporate it into the stitch. Since the bead will come up on the side of your work that's not facing you, you will use this stitch when the wrong side or non-beaded side of your work is facing you.

A reverse beaded single crochet stitch, on the other hand, involves a slightly more awkward twist of the wrist as you insert your hook from back to front. Since the bead will come up on the side of your work facing you, this stitch is worked on right-side rows. In the case of longer beaded reverse stitches (such as the beaded double crochet and beaded triple crochet), you rotate your entire piece after making the stitch to twist the whole stitch around, thereby forcing the bead to show its face on the right side of your work.

Beaded Stitches
Beaded stitches are worked when the non-beaded side of your work is facing you.

Beaded Chain Stitch (bead ch)
Slide 1 bead up the crochet cotton close to hook, yo on the far side of the bead (Photo A), draw crochet cotton through lp on hook.

Photo A

Beaded Single Crochet (bead sc)

Slide 1 bead up the crochet cotton close to hook, insert hook in indicated st, yo on the far side of the bead (Photo B), draw crochet cotton through st, yo and draw through 2 lps on hook.

Photo B

Beaded Double Crochet (bead dc)

Yo, insert hook in indicated st, yo, draw through, yo, draw through 2 lps on hook, slide 1 bead up the crochet cotton close to hook, yo on far side of bead (Photo C), yo and draw through 2 lps on hook.

Photo C

Beaded Treble Crochet (bead tr)

Yo twice, insert hook in indicated st, yo, draw through, [yo, draw through 2 lps on hook] twice, slide 1 bead up the crochet cotton close to hook, yo on far side of bead (Photo D), yo and draw through 2 lps on hook.

Photo D

Beaded Double Treble Crochet (bead dtr)

Yo 3 times, insert hook in indicated st, yo, draw through, [yo, draw through 2 lps on hook] 3 times, slide 1 bead up the crochet cotton close to hook, yo on far side of bead (Photo E), yo and draw through 2 lps on hook.

Photo E

Multi-Beaded Treble Crochet (multi-bead tr)

Yo twice, insert hook in indicated st, yo, draw through, [slide up a bead close to hook, yo on far side of bead, draw through 2 lps on hook] 3 times (Photo F).

Photo F

Reverse Beaded Stitches

Reverse beaded stitches are worked on RS rows, when the beaded side of work is facing you.

Reverse Beaded Single Crochet (reverse bead sc)

Slide 1 bead up close to your hook. Holding crochet cotton and bead to front of hook, move hook down behind the crochet cotton and behind your work; insert it through the base st *from back to front.* Holding hook pointing downward, bring it down onto the crochet cotton on the far side of the bead, yo (Photo G), draw through the st, rolling the hook away from you and up as it comes up behind the st; yo and draw through 2 lps on hook.

Photo G

Reverse Beaded Double Crochet (reverse bead dc)

Work same as a bead dc. Turn work as if turning a page in a book (arrow in Photo H), ch 1, or ch 2 if you crochet very tightly (Photo I). The ch or chs compensate for the tightening that happens when you twist the st. It also serves to leave a place to work into on the next row or rnd.

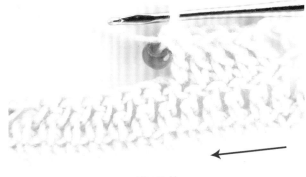

Photo H

Photo I

Reverse Beaded Treble Crochet (reverse bead tr)

Work same as a bead tr. Turn work in same direction as for reverse bead dc. Ch 1, or ch 2 if you crochet very tightly (Photo J). The ch or chs compensate for the tightening that happens when you twist the st. It also serves to leave a place to work into on the next rnd.

Photo J

Reverse Beaded Double Treble Crochet (reverse bead dtr)

Work same as a bead dtr. Turn work in same direction as for reverse bead dc. Ch 1, or ch 2 if you crochet very tightly (Photo K). The ch or chs compensate for the tightening that happens when you twist the st. It also serves to leave a place to work into on the next rnd.

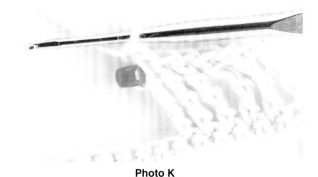

Photo K

Reverse Beaded Triple Treble Crochet (reverse bead trtr)

Yo 4 times, insert hook in indicated st, yo, draw through, [yo, draw through 2 lps on hook] 4 times, slide 1 bead up the crochet cotton close to hook, yo on far side of bead, yo and draw through 2 lps on hook. Turn work completely around (Photo L). Ch 1, or ch 2 if you crochet very tightly. The ch or chs compensate for the tightening that happens when you twist the st. It also serves to leave a place to work into on the next rnd. ■

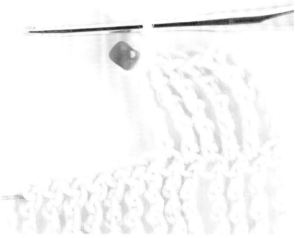

Photo L

BEADED CHAIN LACE EDGING

Dress up plain pairs of flip-flops to go with every summer ensemble in your wardrobe.

Design | Melody MacDuffee

Skill Level

INTERMEDIATE

Finished Size

Approximately ½ inch x desired length

Materials

Size 10 crochet cotton (350 yds per ball):
    1 ball yellow
Size 9/1.25mm steel crochet hook or size needed
    to obtain gauge
Tapestry needle
Multicoloured opaque E beads
Flip-flops
Tacky craft glue

Gauge

1 pattern rep = ½ inch

Chain Lace Edging

Note: String 4 beads for every pattern rep.

Row 1 (RS): Ch 3, sc in 2nd ch from hook and in next ch, turn.

Row 2: Ch 1, sc in each sc, turn.

Row 3: Ch 1, sc in first sc, (**bead sc**—*see General Directions on page 97*, 3 **bead ch**—*see General Directions on page 96*, 2 dc) in next sc, turn.

Row 4: Ch 1, sc in each of first 2 dc, turn.

Next rows: [Rep rows 3 and 4 alternately] for desired length.

Fasten off and weave in ends.

Finishing

To attach Edging to flip-flops, apply glue to straps 1–2 inches at a time and press back side of Edging firmly to strap. Let each section dry for a few minutes or until secure before continuing. ■

Beaded Chain Lace Edging
Sample project was crocheted with Aunt Lydia's Classic Crochet (100 per cent mercerized cotton) from Coats & Clark.

NARROW SHELL LACE EDGING

Turn a plain camisole into a wow *camisole with a beautiful beaded edging.*

Design | Melody MacDuffee

Skill Level

INTERMEDIATE

Finished Size
Approximately ¾ inch x desired length

Materials
Size 10 crochet cotton (300 yds per ball):
    1 ball shaded blues
Size 9/1.25mm steel crochet hook or size needed
   to obtain gauge
Tapestry needle
Dark blue opaque E beads
Camisole
Sewing needle and matching thread *(optional)*
Fabric glue *(optional)*

Gauge
1 pattern rep = 1 inch

Shell Lace Edging

Base
Note: String 5 beads for every pattern rep. Total number of rows worked should be a multiple of 4.

Row 1 (RS): Ch 4, (dc, ch 2, sc) in 4th ch from hook, turn.

Row 2: Ch 3, (dc, ch 2, sc) in next ch-2 sp, turn.

Next rows: Rep row 2 for desired length. At end of last row, **do not turn.**

Beaded Top Edging
Ch 1, working across long edge, sc in side of last sc made, *ch 1, ({**bead tr** (see *General Directions on page 97*), ch 1} 5 times) in sp formed by next beg ch-3, sc in sp formed by next beg ch-3, rep from * to last 2 beg ch-3 sps, ch 1, ({bead tr, ch 1} 5 times) in sp formed by next beg ch-3, sc in first ch of beg ch-4.

Fasten off and weave in ends.

Finishing
To attach Edging to camisole, sew edging to neckline with matching thread, or apply fabric glue around neckline 1–2 inches at a time and press back side of Edging firmly to fabric. Let each section dry for a few minutes or until secure before continuing. ∎

Narrow Shell Lace Edging
Sample project was crocheted with Aunt Lydia's Classic Crochet (100 per cent mercerized cotton) from Coats & Clark.

NARROW BEADED FAN LACE EDGING

Your table will have a new look when you trim your old place setting with a beaded edging.

Design | Melody MacDuffee

Skill Level

INTERMEDIATE

Finished Size

Approximately 1 inch x desired length

Materials

Size 10 crochet cotton (350 yds per ball):
    1 ball each orange (MC) and turquoise (CC)
Size 9/1.25mm steel crochet hook or size needed
    to obtain gauge
Turquoise and orange opaque E beads
Placemat
Contrasting napkin
Sewing needle and matching thread *(optional)*
Fabric glue *(optional)*
Tapestry needle

Gauge

9 sc = 1 inch

Placemat Edging

Note: String 11 beads for every pattern rep.

Row 1 (RS): With MC, ch 10, sc in 2nd ch from hook and in each rem ch across, turn. *(9 sc)*

Row 2: Ch 1, sc in first sc, sk next 3 sc, ({**bead tr**—*see General Directions on page 97,* ch 1} 6 times, bead tr) in next sc *(fan)*, sk next 3 sc, sc in last sc, turn.

Row 3: Ch 8 *(counts as dtr and ch-3 sp)*, sk next 3 bead tr, sc in next bead tr, ch 3, **dtr** *(see Stitch Guide on page 126)* in last sc, turn.

Row 4: Ch 1, sc in first dtr, 3 sc in next ch-3 sp, sc in next sc, 3 sc in sp formed by beg ch-8, sc in 4th ch of same beg ch-8, turn.

Row 5: Ch 1, sc in first sc, [**reverse bead sc** *(see General Directions on page 97)* in next sc, sc in next sc] 4 times, turn.

Next rows: Rep rows 2–5 for desired length, ending last rep with row 4. Fasten off.

Narrow Beaded Fan Lace Edging
Sample project was crocheted with Aunt Lydia's Classic Crochet (100 per cent mercerized cotton) from Coats & Clark.

Finishing

Apply glue along short edge of placemat about 1 inch from left side and press WS of top edge of Edging firmly into it. Let dry for a few minutes until secure. Place a drop of glue on WS of each fan and carefully press to placemat. Glue along bottom edge and press. Let dry. *Note: If preferred, sew trim to placemat with matching thread.*

Napkin Ring

With CC, work same as for Placemat Edging for desired length.

Finishing

Hold piece with RS of short ends tog. With tapestry needle and matching crochet cotton, sew ends tog. ∎

VERTICAL ARCH BEADED FAN LACE EDGING

Turn a plain glass container into a pretty vase just by adding a beaded edging.

Design | Melody MacDuffee

Skill Level

INTERMEDIATE

Finished Size

Approximately ⅞ inch x desired length

Materials

Size 10 crochet cotton (350 yds per ball):
   1 ball pale green
Size 9/1.25mm steel crochet hook or size needed
   to obtain gauge
Dark green opaque E beads
Vase
Tapestry needle

Gauge

Rows 1 and 2 = 1 inch

Special Stitch

Triple treble crochet (trtr): Yo 4 times, draw up lp in st indicated, [yo, draw through 2 lps on hook] 5 times.

Vertical Arch Beaded Fan Lace Edging

Note: String 5 beads for every pattern rep.

Row 1 (RS): Ch 6, tr in 6th ch from hook, turn.

Row 2: Ch 1, sc in first tr, work (sl st, ch 6, tr) in sp formed by beg 5 sk chs, turn.

Row 3: Ch 1, sc in first tr, (sl st, ch 6, tr) in next ch-6 sp, turn.

Next rows: Rep row 3 for desired length, ending with a RS row. At end of last row, **do not turn.**

Border

Working along long edge, (**reverse bead sc, reverse bead dc, reverse bead tr, reverse bead dtr, reverse bead trtr**—see *General Directions on page 98 and 99*, **trtr**—see *Special Stitch*) in sp formed by last tr made, 6 sc in side of trtr just made, ch 2, sk next row, *(reverse bead sc, reverse bead dc, reverse bead tr, reverse bead dtr, reverse bead trtr, trtr) in sp formed by edge tr of next row, 6 sc in side of trtr just made, ch 2, sk next row, rep from * to row 1, (reverse bead sc, reverse bead dc, reverse bead tr, reverse bead dtr, reverse bead trtr) in sp formed by edge tr of row 1, trtr in ch at base of same tr.

Fasten off and weave in ends.

Finishing

To attach Edging to vase, arrange Edging around neck of vase and sew ends tog with tapestry needle and crochet cotton. ■

Vertical Arch Beaded Fan Lace Edging
Sample project was crocheted with Aunt Lydia's
Classic Crochet (100 per cent mercerized cotton)
from Coats & Clark.

LAMPSHADE EDGINGS

Give an old lampshade a new life with this pretty beaded edging.

Design | Melody MacDuffee

Skill Level

INTERMEDIATE

Finished Size

Approximately 1 inch x desired length

Materials

Size 10 crochet cotton (350 yds per ball):
   1 ball brown
Size 9/1.25mm steel crochet hook or size needed
   to obtain gauge
Dark red, peach and orange opaque E beads
Tapestry needle
Lampshade
Tacky craft glue

Gauge

1 pattern rep = ½ inch

Lampshade Edgings

Bottom Edging

Note: String 7 dark red beads, 5 peach beads and 3 orange beads for every pattern rep.

Row 1 (RS): Ch 4, (2 tr, ch 3, hdc) in 4th ch from hook, turn.

Row 2: Ch 3, (2 tr, ch 3, hdc) in next ch-3 sp, turn.

Row 3: In first hdc, work (**bead sc**—*see General Directions on page 97,* sliding 7 beads close to hook; bead sc, sliding 5 beads close to hook; bead sc, sliding 3 beads close to hook), (3 tr, ch 3, hdc) in next ch-3 sp, turn.

Next rows: Rep rows 2 and 3 for desired length. At end of last row, **do not turn.** Fasten off and weave in ends.

Top Edging

Note: String 1 dark red bead, 1 peach bead and 1 orange bead for every pattern rep.

Rows 1 and 2: Rep rows 1 and 2 of Bottom Edging.

Row 3: Bead sc in first hdc, sliding 3 beads close to hook, (3 tr, ch 3, hdc) in next ch-3 sp, turn.

Next rows: Rep rows 2 and 3 for desired length. At end of last row, do not turn. Fasten off and weave in ends.

Finishing

To assemble Edging, tie ends of Bottom Edging tog and weave in ends. Rep with ends of Top Edging. Apply glue along bottom edge of lampshade 1–2 inches at a time and press back side of Edging firmly into it. Let each section dry for a few minutes until secure before continuing. Attach Top Edging to top edge of lampshade in same manner. ∎

Lampshade Edgings

Sample project was crocheted with Aunt Lydia's Classic Crochet (100 per cent mercerized cotton) from Coats & Clark.

TRIANGLES IN LACE

Add to the elegance of your bedroom with this fabulous pillowcase edging.

Design | Sharon Valiant

Skill Level
INTERMEDIATE

Finished Size
3 inches x desired length

Materials
Size 10 crochet cotton (350 yds per ball):
    1 ball gold
Size 7/1.65mm steel crochet hook or size needed
   to obtain gauge
Sewing needle and matching thread
Pillowcase

Gauge
10 dc = 1 inch

Notes
For 2¼-inch Edging, use size 20 crochet cotton and size 9/1.25mm steel crochet hook.

For 1¾-inch Edging, use size 30 crochet cotton and size 11/1.10mm steel crochet hook.

Special Stitches
Shell: (3 dc, ch 2, 3 dc) in place indicated.

Double shell: (3 dc, {ch 2, 3 dc} twice) in place indicated.

Triangles Edging

Row 1: Ch 5, **shell** *(see Special Stitches)* in 5th ch from hook, turn.

Row 2: Ch 7, shell in ch-2 sp of shell, turn.

Row 3: Ch 3, shell in ch-2 sp of shell, ch 3, **double shell** *(see Special Stitches)* in ch-7 sp, turn.

Row 4: Ch 8, [shell in next ch-2 sp, ch 4] twice, sk next ch-3 sp, dc in each of next 3 dc, shell in ch-2 sp of shell, turn.

Row 5: Ch 3, shell in ch-2 sp of next shell, dc in each of next 6 dc, ch 4, shell in ch-2 sp of next shell, ch 2, shell in next ch-4 sp, ch 2, shell in ch-2 sp of next shell, turn.

Row 6: Ch 8, [shell in ch-2 sp of next shell, ch 3] twice, shell in ch-2 sp of next shell, ch 4, dc in each of next 9 dc, shell in ch-2 sp of next shell, turn.

Row 7: Ch 3, shell in ch-2 sp of next shell, dc in each of next 12 dc, [ch 4, shell in ch-2 sp of next shell] 3 times, turn.

Row 8: Ch 8, [[(3 dc, {ch 3, sl st in last dc, 3 dc} twice) in next ch-2 sp of next shell, ch 2, sc in next ch-4 sp, ch 2] twice, ({3 dc, ch 3, sl st in last dc} twice, 3 dc) in ch-2 sp of next shell, ch 4, dc in each of next 15 dc, shell in ch-2 sp of next shell, turn.

Triangles in Lace
Sample project was crocheted with Aunt Lydia's Classic Crochet (100 per cent mercerized cotton) from Coats & Clark.

Row 9: Ch 3, shell in ch-2 sp of next shell, leaving rem sts unworked, turn.

Row 10: Ch 7, shell in ch-2 sp of next shell, turn.

Row 11: Ch 3, shell in ch-2 sp of next shell, ch 3, double shell in next ch-7 sp, ch 4, sk 5 dc of 18-dc group, sl st in next dc, turn.

Row 12: Ch 4, [shell in next ch-2 sp, ch 4] twice, sk next ch-3 sp, dc in each of next 3 dc, shell in ch-2 sp of next shell, turn.

Row 13: Ch 3, shell in ch-2 sp of next shell, dc in each of next 6 dc, ch 4, shell in ch-2 sp of next shell, ch 2, shell in next ch-4 sp, ch 2, shell in ch-2 sp of next shell, ch 4, sk next 5 dc of 18-dc group, sl st in next dc, turn.

Row 14: Ch 4, [shell in ch-2 sp of next shell, ch 3] twice, shell in ch-2 sp of next shell, ch 4, dc in each of next 9 dc, shell in ch-2 sp of shell, turn.

Row 15: Ch 3, shell in ch-2 sp of next shell, dc in each of next 12 dc, [ch 4, shell in ch-2 sp of next shell] 3 times, ch 4, sk next 5 dc of 18-dc group, sl st in last dc, turn.

Row 16: Ch 4, *({3 dc, ch 3, sl st in last dc} twice, 3 dc) in ch-2 sp of next shell, ch 2, sc in next ch-4 sp, ch 2, rep from * once, ({3 dc, ch 3, sl st in last dc} twice, 3 dc) in ch-2 sp of next shell, ch 4, dc in each of next 15 dc, shell in ch-2 sp of last shell, turn.

Next rows: [Rep rows 9–16 consecutively] until piece measures desired length, ending last rep with row 16.

Top Trim

Row 1 (RS): Turn to work across top edge, ch 1, sc in first st, (3 dc, ch 3, sl st in last dc made) in next ch-3 sp and in each ch-3 sp across. Fasten off.

Finishing

With sewing needle and matching thread, sew Edging to pillowcase as desired. ■

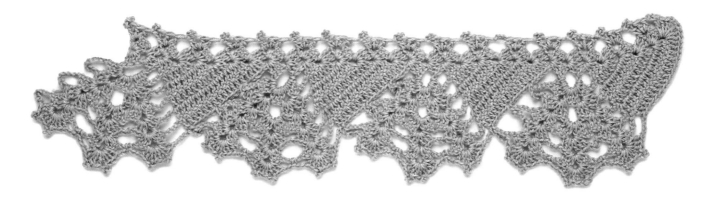

ROWS OF PINEAPPLES

Dress up a purchased tablecloth with this beautiful insertion or edging.

Design | Sharon Valiant

Skill Level
EASY

Finished Size
3½ inches x desired length

Materials
Size 10 crochet cotton (350 yds per ball):
    1 ball olive green
Size 7/1.65mm steel crochet hook or size needed
    to obtain gauge
Sewing needle and matching thread
Tablecloth

Gauge
Rows 1–6 = 2 inches

Notes
For 2¾-inch Edging, use size 20 crochet cotton and size 9/1.25mm steel crochet hook.

For 2-inch Edging, use size 30 crochet cotton and size 11/1.10mm steel crochet hook.

Special Stitch
Shell: (2 dc, ch 2, 2 dc) in indicated st or sp.

Pineapples Edging

Row 1: Ch 20, **shell** *(see Special Stitch)* in 8th ch from hook, ch 7, sk next 4 chs, sc in next ch, ch 3, sk next ch, sc in next ch, ch 7, sk next 4 chs, shell in next ch, turn.

Row 2: Ch 7, shell in ch sp of first shell, ch 4, sc in next ch-7 sp, ch 5, sc in next ch-7 sp, ch 4, shell in ch sp of last shell, turn.

Row 3: Ch 7, shell in ch sp of first shell, ch 1, 9 tr in ch-5 sp, ch 1, shell in ch sp of last shell, turn.

Row 4: Ch 7, shell in ch sp of first shell, ch 3, sc in next tr, [ch 3, sk next tr, sc in next tr] 4 times, ch 3, shell in ch sp of last shell, turn.

Row 5: Ch 7, shell in ch sp of first shell, ch 4, sk next ch-3 sp, [sc in next ch-3 sp, ch 3] 3 times, ch 3, shell in ch sp of last shell, turn.

Row 6: Ch 7, shell in ch sp of first shell, ch 5, sk next ch-4 sp, [sc in next ch-3 sp, ch 3] twice, sc in next ch-3 sp, ch 5, shell in ch sp of last shell, turn.

Row 7: Ch 7, shell in ch sp of first shell, ch 7, sk ch-5 sp, sc in next ch-3 sp, ch 3, sc in next ch-3 sp, ch 7, shell in ch sp of last shell, turn.

Next rows: [Rep rows 2–7 consecutively] until piece measures desired length.

Last row: Ch 7, shell in ch sp of first shell, ch 5, sk next ch-7 sp, tr in ch-3 sp, ch 5, shell in ch sp of last shell.

Top Trim

Row 1: Turn to work across long edge, sl st in end of next row, ch 8, [sc in next ch-7 sp, ch 5] across to last ch sp, sc in last ch sp, turn.

Row 2: Ch 1, 5 sc in first ch-5 sp and in each ch-5 sp across to last ch-5 sp, 4 sc in last ch-5 sp, sc in 3rd ch of beg ch-8, turn.

Row 3: Ch 5 *(counts as first dc and ch-2)*, [sk next 2 sc, dc in next sc, ch 2] across to last st, dc in last st, turn.

Row 4: Ch 1, [2 sc in ch-2 sp, ch 3] across to beg ch-5, sc in 3rd ch of beg ch-5. Fasten off.

Bottom Trim

Row 1: Join with sc in first ch-7 sp on opposite edge, ch 5, [sc in next ch-7 sp, ch 5] across to last ch sp, sc in last ch sp, turn.

Row 2: Ch 1, 5 sc in first ch-5 sp and in each ch-5 sp across to last ch-5 sp, 4 sc in last ch-5 sp, sc in last st, turn.

Row 3: Ch 5 *(counts as first dc and ch-2)*, [sk next 2 sc, dc in next sc, ch 2] across to last st, dc in last st, turn.

Row 4: Ch 1, [2 sc in next ch-2 sp, ch 3] across, sc in 3rd ch of beg ch-5. Fasten off.

Finishing

Referring to photo for insertions, cut tablecloth into three sections, hem raw edges, and sew Edgings between cut-and-hemmed edges. Or sew Edging to tablecloth as desired. ∎

Rows of Pineapples

Sample project was crocheted with Aunt Lydia's Classic Crochet (100 per cent mercerized cotton) from Coats & Clark.

MILE-A-MINUTE EDGING

Wrap your favourite newborn in a blanket accented with a quick-to-work edging.

Design | Annie Potter

Skill Level

INTERMEDIATE

Finished Size
1¼ inches x desired length

Materials
Size 10 crochet cotton (350 yds per ball):
    1 ball pale blue
Size 7/1.65mm steel crochet hook or size needed
    to obtain gauge
Sewing needle and matching thread
Baby blanket

Gauge
4 rows = 1½ inches

Note
Chain-3 at beginning of row counts as first treble crochet unless otherwise stated.

Special Stitch
Open shell: (Tr, {ch 2, tr} 3 times) in place indicated.

Mile-a-Minute Edging

Row 1: Ch 6, tr in 4th ch from hook *(first 4 chs count as first tr)*, sk next ch, **open shell** *(see Special Stitch)* in last ch, turn.

Row 2: Ch 5, open shell in centre ch-2 sp of open shell, ch 1, tr in each of last 2 sts, turn.

Row 3: Ch 3 *(see Note)*, tr in next st, ch 1, open shell in centre ch-2 sp of next open shell, turn.

Next rows: [Rep rows 2 and 3 alternately] until edging reaches desired length. At end of last row, fasten off.

Finishing
With sewing needle and matching thread, sew Edging around edge of blanket. ∎

Mile-a-Minute Edging
Sample project was crocheted with Aunt Lydia's Classic Crochet (100 per cent mercerized cotton) from Coats & Clark.

FORGET-ME-NOT EDGING

A pretty floral edging can really dress up an everyday dish towel.

Design | Delsie Rhoades

Skill Level
EASY

Finished Size
Approximately 2 inches by desired length
(1 rep is about 2 inches long)

Materials
Size 10 crochet cotton (ecru: 225 yds per ball; light blue: 150 yds per ball):
    1 ball each ecru (MC) and light blue (CC)
Size 5/1.90mm steel crochet hook or size needed to obtain gauge
Sewing needle and matching thread
Dish towel

Gauge
8 dc = 1 inch

Special Stitch
Cluster (cl): Keeping last lp of each dc on hook, 3 dc in st indicated, yo and draw through all 4 lps on hook.

Forget-Me-Not Edging

Flower
Note: Make 1 flower for each 2 inches of length desired.

Rnd 1: With CC, ch 2, 6 sc in 2nd ch from hook, join in first sc.

Rnd 2: Ch 3, (**cl**—*see Special Stitch*, ch 3, sl st) in same sc as beg ch-3 *(beg petal)*, *(sl st, ch 3, cl, ch 3, sl st) in next sc *(petal)*, rep from * 4 times. *(6 petals)*

Fasten off.

Edging
Row 1: Hold 1 Flower with RS facing, join MC in any cl, ch 6, [sl st in next cl, ch 6] twice, *sl st in any cl of next Flower, ch 6, [sl st in next cl, ch 6] twice, rep from * to last Flower, sl st in any cl of last Flower, [ch 6, sl st in next cl] twice, turn.

Row 2: Sl st in next ch-6 sp, ch 1, sc in same sp, ch 6, sc in next ch-6 sp, *ch 6, (sc, ch 6, sc) in next ch-6 sp, [ch 6, sc in next ch-6 sp] twice, rep from * across, turn.

Row 3: Sl st in next ch-6 sp, ch 4 *(counts as dc and ch-1 sp)*, dc in same sp, ch 1, *({dc, ch 1} twice) in next ch-6 sp, rep from * to last ch-6 sp, (dc, ch 1, dc) in last sp. **Do not turn.**

Forget-Me-Not Edging
Sample project was crocheted with Aunt Lydia's Classic Crochet (100 per cent mercerized cotton) from Coats & Clark.

Rnd 4: Now working in rnds around entire piece, ch 6, sl st in same cl as last sl st of row 1 of Edging, ch 6, continuing around Flowers along unworked edge of petals, *[sl st in next cl, ch 6] 4 times, sc in ch sp between next 2 sc on Edging, ch 6, sl in next petal on next Flower (where joined to Edging), ch 6, rep from * to last Flower, [sl st in next cl, ch 6] 4 times, sl st in 3rd ch of beg ch-4 of Row 3 and in next ch-1 sp, ch 1, sc in same sp, **ch 3, sc in next ch-1 sp, rep from ** across row 3, join in first ch of beg ch-6.

Fasten off and weave in ends.

Finishing
With sewing needle and matching thread, sew Edging to dish towel as desired. ∎

DAFFODIL EDGING

A pretty edging around a candle makes a nice gift.

Design | Delsie Rhoades

Skill Level

EASY

Finished Size

Approximately 2¼ inches by desired length
(1 rep is about 2 inches long)

Materials

Size 10 crochet cotton (white: 225 yds per ball; shaded yellows: 150 yds per ball):
  1 ball each white (MC) and shaded yellows (CC)
Size 5/1.90mm steel crochet hook or size needed to obtain gauge
Tapestry needle
Candle

Gauge

8 dc = 1 inch

Special Stitch

Cluster (cl): Keeping last lp of each dc on hook, 3 dc in st indicated, yo and draw through all 4 lps on hook.

Daffodil Edging

Flower

Note: Make 1 Flower for each 2 inches of length desired.

Rnd 1: With CC, ch 2, 6 sc in 2nd ch from hook, join in **back lp** *(see Stitch Guide on page 126)* of first sc.

Rnd 2: Ch 3, (**cl**—*see Special Stitch*, ch 3, sl st) in same lp as beg ch-3 *(beg petal)*, working in back lps only, *(sl st, ch 3, cl, ch 3, sl st) in next sc *(petal)*, rep from * 4 times, join in **front lp** *(see Stitch Guide on page 126)* of first sc on rnd 1. *(6 petals)*

Rnd 3: Ch 1, 2 sc in same lp, working in front lps only of rnd 1, 2 sc in each rem lp, join in first sc. *(12 sc)*

Rnd 4: Ch 1, sc in same sc, ch 3, sk next sc, *sc in next sc, ch 3, sk next sc, rep from * around, join in first sc. Fasten off.

Edging

Rnd 1: Join MC in any petal of 1 Flower, ch 8 *(counts as dc and ch-5 sp)*, dc in same sp as beg ch-8, ch 5, [dc, ch 5] twice in next petal, *[dc, ch 5] twice in any petal of next Flower, [dc, ch 5] twice in next petal, rep from * until all Flowers have been joined, dc in next petal on last Flower, ch 5, working across unworked edge of Flowers, [sc in next petal, ch 5] twice, dc in next petal, **dc in next petal on next Flower, ch 5, [sc in next petal, ch 5] twice, dc in next petal, rep from ** across, ch 5, join in 3rd ch of beg ch-8.

Rnd 2: Sl st in next ch-5 sp, ch 1, 3 sc in same sp, *(3 dc, ch 4, sl st in 3rd ch from hook, ch 1, 3 dc) in next ch-5 sp *(picot shell)*, 3 sc in next ch-5 sp, rep from * across top of Flowers, **({sc, ch 3} 3 times) in next ch-5 sp, sc in same sp, rep from ** across bottom of Flowers, join in first sc.

Fasten off and weave in all ends.

Finishing
Sew ends of Edging tog with matching crochet cotton to fit around candle. ■

INDEX

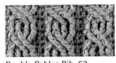

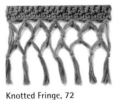

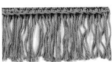

INDEX

GENERAL INFORMATION

Standard Yarn Weight System

Categories of yarn, gauge ranges and recommended needle and hook sizes

Yarn Weight Symbol & Category Names	1 SUPER FINE	2 FINE	3 LIGHT	4 MEDIUM	5 BULKY	6 SUPER BULKY
Type of Yarns in Category	Sock, Fingering, Baby	Sport, Baby	DK, Light Worsted	Worsted, Afghan, Aran	Chunky, Craft, Rug	Super Chunky, Roving
Crochet Gauge* Ranges in Single Crochet to 4 inch	21–32 sts	16–20 sts	12–17 sts	11–14 sts	8–11 sts	5–9 sts
Recommended Hook in Metric Size Range	2.25–3.5mm	3.5–4.5mm	4.5–5.5mm	5.5–6.5mm	6.5–9mm	9mm and larger
Recommended Hook U.S. Size Range	1/B–4/E	4/E–7	7–9/I	9/I–10½/K	10½/K–13/M	13/M and larger

* GUIDELINES ONLY: The above reflect the most commonly used gauges and hooks sizes for specific yarn categories.

Skill Levels

BEGINNER

Beginner projects for first-time crocheters using basic stitches. Minimal shaping.

EASY

Easy projects using basic stitches, repetitive stitch patterns, simple colour changes and simple shaping and finishing.

INTERMEDIATE

Intermediate projects with a variety of stitches, mid-level shaping and finishing.

EXPERIENCED

Experienced projects using advanced techniques and stitches, detailed shaping and refined finishing.

Metric Conversion Charts

METRIC CONVERSIONS

yards   x   .9144   =   metres (m)

yards   x   91.44   =   centimetres (cm)

inches   x   2.54   =   centimetres (cm)

inches   x   25.40   =   millimetres (mm)

inches   x   .0254   =   metres (m)

centimetres   x   .3937   =   inches

metres   x   1.0936   =   yards

INCHES INTO MILLIMETRES & CENTIMETRES (Rounded off slightly)

inches	mm	cm	inches	cm	inches	cm	inches	cm
1/8	3	0.3	5	12.5	21	53.5	38	96.5
1/4	6	0.6	5 1/2	14.0	22	56.0	39	99.0
3/8	10	1.0	6	15.0	23	58.5	40	101.5
1/2	13	1.3	7	18.0	24	61.0	41	104.0
5/8	15	1.5	8	20.5	25	63.5	42	106.5
3/4	20	2.0	9	23.0	26	66.0	43	109.0
7/8	22	2.2	10	25.5	27	68.5	44	112.0
1	25	2.5	11	28.0	28	71.0	45	114.5
1 1/4	32	3.2	12	30.5	29	73.5	46	117.0
1 1/2	38	3.8	13	33.0	30	76.0	47	119.5
1 3/4	45	4.5	14	35.5	31	79.0	48	122.0
2	50	5.0	15	38.0	32	81.5	49	124.5
2 1/2	65	6.5	16	40.5	33	84.0	50	127.0
3	75	7.5	17	43.0	34	86.5		
3 1/2	90	9.0	18	46.0	35	89.0		
4	100	10.0	19	48.5	36	91.5		
4 1/2	115	11.5	20	51.0	37	94.0		

KNITTING NEEDLES CONVERSION CHART

U.S.	0	1	2	3	4	5	6	7	8	9	10	10½	11	13	15
Canada/U.K.	14	13	12	10	-	9	8	7	6	5	4	3	0	00	000
Metric (mm)	2	2.25	2.75	3.25	3.5	3.75	4	4.5	5	5.5	6	6.5	8	9	10

CROCHET HOOKS CONVERSION CHART

U.S.	1/B	2/C	3/D	4/E	5/F	6/G	8/H	9/I	10/J	10½/K	15/N
Canada/U.K.	13	-	10	9	-	8	6	5	4	3	000
Metric (mm)	2.25	2.75	3.25	3.5	3.75	4	5	5.5	6	6.5	10

STITCH GUIDE

Chain (ch): Yo, pull through lp on hook.

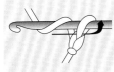

Slip stitch (sl st): Insert hook in st, pull through both lps on hook.

Front loop (front lp) Back loop (back lp)

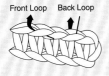

Front Loop   Back Loop

Single crochet (sc): Insert hook in st, yo, pull through st, yo, pull through both lps on hook.

Front post stitch (fp): Back post stitch (bp): When working post st, insert hook from right to left around post of st on previous row.

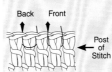

Back   Front

Post of Stitch

Half double crochet (hdc): Yo, insert hook in st, yo, pull through st, yo, pull through all 3 lps on hook.

Double treble crochet (dtr): Yo 3 times, insert hook in st, yo, pull through st, [yo, pull through 2 lps] 4 times.

Change colours: Drop first colour; with 2nd colour, pull through last 2 lps of st.

Double crochet (dc): Yo, insert hook in st, yo, pull through st, [yo, pull through 2 lps] twice.

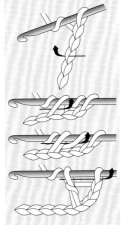

Treble crochet (tr): Yo twice, insert hook in st, yo, pull through st, [yo, pull through 2 lps] 3 times.

Single crochet decrease (sc dec): (Insert hook, yo, draw lp through) in each of the sts indicated, yo, draw through all lps on hook.

Example of 2-sc dec

Half double crochet decrease (hdc dec): (Yo, insert hook, yo, draw lp through) in each of the sts indicated, yo, draw through all lps on hook.

Example of 2-hdc dec

Double crochet decrease (dc dec): (Yo, insert hook, yo, draw lp through, yo, draw through 2 lps on hook) in each of the sts indicated, yo, draw through all lps on hook.

Example of 2-dc dec

Example of 2-tr dec

Treble crochet decrease (tr dec): Holding back last lp of each st, tr in each of the sts indicated, yo, pull through all lps on hook.

US		UK
sl st (slip stitch)	=	sc (single crochet)
sc (single crochet)	=	dc (double crochet)
hdc (half double crochet)	=	htr (half treble crochet)
dc (double crochet)	=	tr (treble crochet)
tr (treble crochet)	=	dtr (double treble crochet)
dtr (double treble crochet)	=	ttr (triple treble crochet)
skip	=	miss

GOT A PASSION FOR CRAFTING?

Each craft pattern book offers unique designs, easy-to-follow instructions, helpful how-to illustrations and full-colour photos—all for a very low price! Get creative and start a beautiful new project today for yourself or a loved one.

Crocheting Slippers
Crocheting Slippers provides 18 delightful patterns for cute and cozy slippers to keep the whole family's toes toasty. A handy stitch guide helps you put together these creative designs.

Crocheting Toys
In an age where so many things are mass-produced, the craft of crochet allows you to custom-create a toy or game for that special little one. These handcrafted toys will quickly become favourites and heartfelt reminders in years to come.

Quilting Pot Holders
Add flare to your kitchen with 45 unique designs for handy pot holders—you're sure to find something to suit any taste! *Quilting Pot Holders* includes full-colour photos of each project, useful instructions, templates and patterns.

Knitting for Dogs
Dogs are beloved members of our families, so of course we want to make them feel important with their own sweaters, beds and comfort toys. These fun designs will be a perfect match for your four-footed friend.

Sewing Aprons
Like to cook and love to sew? Just select one of our easy designs for fun and funky aprons that will keep your clothes clean while you're busy in the kitchen or the garden. Start sewing now, and stitch one for yourself or for a special friend!

Knitting Winter Accessories
Keep toasty warm when the cold winds blow with this great collection of knitted accessories. You'll find cozy hats, classy scarves, plus mittens and fingerless gloves. It's time to start knitting for a warm winter ahead.